Aging

Its History and Literature

Joseph T. Freeman, M.D., F.A.C.P.

HUMAN SCIENCES PRESS
72 Fifth Avenue   3 Henrietta Street
NEW YORK, NY 10011 ● LONDON, WC2E 8LU

Library of Congress Catalog Number 79-11839
ISBN: 0-87705-251-4

Copyright © 1979 by Human Sciences Press
72 Fifth Avenue, New York, New York 10011

Printed in the United States of America
9 987654321

Library of Congress Cataloging in Publication Data

Freeman, Joseph T
  Aging's history and literature.

  Includes index
    1. Gerontology—History. 2. Geriatrics—History.
  3. Gerontology—Bibliography. 4. Geriatrics—Bibliography. I. Title.
  HQ1061.F713   016.30143'5'09   79-11839
  ISBN 0-87705-251-4

RECOGNITION ...

For out of the old fieldes, as men saieth,
Commeth al this new corne, fro yere to yere,
And out of old bookes, in good faieth,
Commeth all this new science that men lere.
But now to purpose, ...

... Geoffrey Chaucer

> The Assemblie of Foules, *in*
> *The Workes of our Ancient and*
> *learned English Poet, Geffrey*
> *Chaucer,* by Frauncis Beaumont
> London, printed by Adam Islip, 1602

REMEMBERING ...

Clive McCay
Walter Kahoe
George Kern

Contents

Introduction

$\mathcal{T}$he material for gerontology's history, literature, and documentation for the most part has accumulated in haphazard fashion. The major body of work has not been organized in a way that is serviceable for the increasing number of students of all aspects of aging. Exceptions must be noted for some distinguished efforts at documentation but even these are scattered through the usual indexes, often in unclassified fashion. Most of the publications have been the product of a few individuals who have had little support and less financial assistance. These dedicated efforts rarely are known among many workers in social, clinical, and humanistic areas. However, organization began to be introduced by the mid-part of the 20th century.

Coordination, cataloguing, and classification of the literature of aging is essential to identify what has been accomplished and to know what contributions are available to enrich current studies. The most cursory review of new titles and opinions shows how laboriously the subject is reworked and how much effort could have been eliminated, or made more valid, if there had been recourse to the observations of earlier advocates, many of whom were perceptive, literate, and foresightful. In short, knowledge of gerontology's bibliography prior to 1950 generally is inadequate for the needs of the field.

The first effort to prepare a proper compilation was done by the industrious and prolific John Sinclair of Edinburgh* who received a baronetcy for his many contributions to statistics, agriculture, parliament, and aging among other publicized interests. In four volumes published in 1804, entitled *The Code of Longevity,* he brought together a great deal of material that included résumés of classical authors, letters from scientists and friends, pictures of aging people, a variety of analyses, and a compendium of almost 2000 titles. Von Haller and Choulant contributed in their time to the bibliography of aging.[1] A major review was published by Carl Canstatt in 1839, and Charcot in 1867 added a dramatic chapter of historic content in his published volume of lectures.

With the emergence of the terms *gerontology* and *geriatrics* in the 20th century, both significant of the growing application to the biological and clinical aspects of senescence, parallel interest in historical documents developed and was made available in a series of fine papers and monographs by a half dozen historians. A majority of them were physicians.

The Gerontological Society of the United States was aware in the 1960s of the need to document the subject. It created a Documentation Committee that became its Documentation and History of Gerontology Committee. Less than a decade later, the International Association of

---

*Names of many authors have not been given reference numbers because their identification appears later in listings of the monograph and will be included in the name index of authors. The few that are not identified in this way will be numbered in the usual bibliographic form, and also will appear in the index of authors' names.

Gerontology accepted a proposal to create a History of Gerontology Committee.

Organized data collection by computer methods began about the same time. Listings of aging under a variety of headings have been known, aside from the private bibliographies, from the first volume of the *Index Catalogue of the Library of the Surgeon-General's Office*, 1879, and its successors with rubrics of increasing specificity. A special effort by a scientific society's publication began in tabular form in the first issue of the *Journal of Gerontology* in 1946. In short order, this effort was organized superbly in classified form and continues with each journal's issue later compiled into several bound volumes as *A Classified Bibliography of Gerontology and Geriatrics*, edited by Nathan W. Shock; the first supplement covered 1949–1955.

A number of gerontology's historians have written about pioneer observers, research trends, and historical evaluations of the study of aging from remote times. Historical analysis lagged behind the collections of narratives and annals. Current developments, guaranteed by a flow of funds and stimulated by the National Institute on Aging's rapport with the National Library of Medicine, will contribute to the documentation of the current literature of aging. Retrievals from the past should be a useful adjunct.

Strangely enough, many historians and some teachers of general science have been untouched by, and even uninformed of, the history of aging to the point that they profess surprise when exposed to the amount of material that is available. The quality and quantity of a good deal of the finished work seem to have remained outside of the main channel of the science's historiography. At a time when aging has become a most important topic in affluent nations with major influences on national economics and political direction, much of the data lacks the professional dedication and endorsement that can be brought to policies by a consideration of what is in library stacks. The world of ideas, it seems, has been satisfied merely by the recollections and reminiscences of newly arrived econo-mists and sociologists. Many of them have not had an ex-posure to the prime views on aging that should but failed to have an impact on modern actions, so that the splendid efforts of the past rest in stacks seldom used to reflect on current needs.

The word aging has shown a tendency to be denigratory in itself. Self-identification can be a motivating force but also may be a negative one. An occasional book, of which Simone de Beauvoir's *Coming of Age* is a good example, might ruffle complacency for a bit but its origin seems to be an expression of the author's needs to spell out personal awareness of what is happening to the life and career of a talented writer rather than an objective evaluation of major social import.

Repetitive translations of Cicero's *De Senectute* in re-prints of works on old age, or interest stimulated by a variety of claims for rejuvenatory processes, always are popular. But recourse, and access, to the substantive litera-ture of sound concepts and the development of ideas about aging have been neglected, even by serious students. At the same time, there has been a rising interest in and sometimes a weary repetition of studies in which physi-ologic capacities are evaluated and revealed and quantita-tive estimations that began as long ago as the 17th century finally achieve precise measurements. Gerontology re-quires this type of quantitation.

When did the figure of a gerontologist emerge to assume a lien on a particular part of the life scene? Was it a biology student who was self-bound to the study of the aging process and sometimes subspecied as a geriatric clinician? Was it foresight that saw more of life becoming assured of a long trek into old age? Was it a need to under-stand, but not to placate, that the elder years must be put into perspective of undisclosed but unquestioned values and integrity? The questions raise a question in reply. Can the finite mind accept the finite body, young and old, that has benefited by all that has gone before in human events leaving to the infinite that which could not be altered in biologic terms and is to be taken on faith as the alternative?

Gerontology grew enough in the last trimester of the 20th century to appreciate that it is being engaged, and has to be engaged if the science has meaning, in one of the major debates of the times. Old bodies are being dismantled in terms of their age like parts of a clock strewn on a table top in an effort to understand the *mechanisms of time* in order to arrive at an understanding of its *being* in time.

It is without question that aging's history and literature are being studied avidly and are forcing their results into consciousness. The amount of the works of the past is beyond the resources of most students to find or to read. Selectivity and abbreviation will help to bridge the past and present. In selected chapters, it becomes possible to be exposed to the thoughts of major contributors with a minimum of effort and possibly a great deal of benefit.

In order to afford a sound basis for such efforts, a number of works have been classified under headings covering much of the data from the first three quarters of the 20th century. The chapters have been entitled:

1. The History of Gerocomy, Gerontology, and Geriatrics: A Résumé
2. 100 Distinguished Works on Aging, Old Age, and the Aged
3. The Historiology of Gerontology's Historiographers: A Classified Bibliography, 1900–1975
4. Classified List of Journals on Aging, Old Age, and the Aged to 1975

Collectively they represent a documentation of modern gerontology in its present state with overtones about aging that will not accept a secondary status for this stage of life as if it were some nondescript fraction of the population to be treated as a laboratory cohort rather than with the dignity of people enacting a unique role in the third trimester, or period, of life after age 65.

REFERENCE

1. Choulant JL: Handbuch der Bückerkunde für die Ältere Medicin. Leipzig, L Voss, 1828

1

The History of Gerocomy, Gerontology, and Geriatrics: A Résumé

INTRODUCTION

The historical method is based on the "need to know all the strong fortresses of the spirit which men have built through the ages." Mankind's compounded experiences must not be left secluded and neglected in silent sanctuaries.[1] In every human quest, the hope of survival and the urgency to achieve an understanding of old age are important parts of science's historical imperatives.

"One hallmark of a civilized society," it was said, "is its willingness to care for its poor, ill, elderly ... and handicapped." *Saturday Review* (May 1970) Awareness of the nature of old age and the needs of the aging have a long lineage. The modern era began in 1909 when Ignatius Leo Nascher of New York coined the word *geriatrics* for the clinical aspects of aging. Six years before that time, in 1903, according to Gruman, Metchnikoff at the Pasteur Institute in Paris invented the term *gerontology* for the biologic study of senescence. *Gerocomy* was used by Galen in the 1st century A.D. for the medical care of the elderly and now is promoted as a designation of their sociology.[2] Nascher's book was published in 1914 and with it the clinical study of aging became definitive.

Guidelines for the behavior of humanity were transmitted verbally from generation to generation before rules of conduct were inscribed. With these written records that summarized the lessons of the past, ancient laws became sanctified and often were credited as being inspired divinely. Taboos that governed the lives of persons and groups became religious dogma supported particularly by the elders who were prime beneficiaries. Parental respect in life and death was a commandment. Councils were made up of elders. Rules of property and inheritance supported the authority of the old. It took the major upheavals of war, starvation, epidemic diseases, and youthful rebellion to overthrow a gerontocracy that could be oppressive. In most of the written works that appeared in monolithic civilizations as much as 3000 years before the Christian Era, roles of the old and rules for medical care were listed.

At least 9 periods in the scientific knowledge of old age from the beginning of recorded history to the present can be defined in the last 5000 years.

Fig. 1

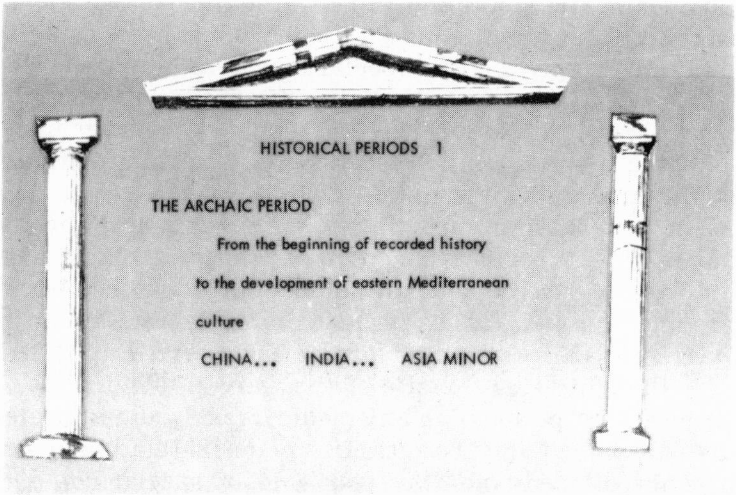

HISTORICAL PERIODS 1

THE ARCHAIC PERIOD

From the beginning of recorded history

to the development of eastern Mediterranean

culture

CHINA... INDIA... ASIA MINOR

Heading, 1st historical section.

ARCHAIC PERIOD

The Archaic Period extended from the beginning of literate records to the emergence of the great eastern Mediterranean and Asian cultures.

These ancient civilizations bore the hallmarks of their patriarchs in which aging personified achievement. Three cultural areas left records of their codes that have been identified. China, India, and the land bridge from the

Indus River to Egypt that included Persian, Assyrian, Chaldean, Mesopotamian, and Dalmunic contributions were seedbeds of mankind's laws. In each of these centers there were expressions of special considerations of the old with few variations over the centuries. In China and India rules for the old largely were parochial and either unadaptable or unacceptable elsewhere because of unique qualities expressive of national philosophies.

The Code of Hammurabi who was the king of Babylon about 2250 B.C. is given the credit of priority in mankind's regulation "based upon a still older source, and is a legal document, which makes it clear that a definite medical class existed in the Valley of the Tigris and Euphrates [also thought to be the site of the Garden of Eden] at a much earlier period than any medical text would indicate of themselves." The Code contains material relating to the practice of medicine "but was void of special content about the old.[3] This "first historical codification of medicine"[4] was carved on a stele of dioritic stone on the other side of which was the portrait of the Babylonian king paying devotion to the sun-god worshipped as the source of royal origin and inspiration. These ancient and useful lines became the roots of humanism with directives in religion, health care, and human conduct.

Far removed in distance but at about the same time in history, the Emperor Huang-ti of the Han Dynasty ordered the compilation of his socratic interviews with his sages known as the *Nei Ching Su Wên* or *The Yellow Emperor's Classic of Internal Medicine* described as a "classic treatise on internal medicine, and supposedly the oldest medical book extant."[5] The emperor lived 100 years from 2697 to 2597 B.C. Disturbances in physiologic balance were blamed for aging and death. In the view of Tao, or the Way, there was a unity in nature expressed in the opposing principles of Yin and Yang. Taoism included a concept of longevity in which life was to be extended in good health and old age was portrayed vividly. In the 19th chapter of the 6th book the observation was made that "when man grows old, his bones become brittle ... his flesh sags ... there is gas within the thorax resulting in labored breathing ... the limit of man's life can be perceived when man can no longer overcome his diseases."[5] When harmony exists, health and longevity merge; the expressions of the aging process were seen as a disease.

In India, Sushruta, disciple of Dhanvantari, was said to be "the first propounder of medical science on earth."[6] The body was recognized as the possessor of "innate morbific tendencies" that limited life-span naturally. The similarity between the Indian views and Hippocratic aphorisms suggested the influence of the earlier culture on Greek thought possibly transmitted by Pythagoras. In the 7th century translation of Sushruta into Arabic and then into Latin it was claimed that "the basis of all systems of scientific medicines in the world" are assumed to have dated from India; much of European medicine was based on this Latin version.[3] Very precise measurements were given for body aging. Medications such as Soma and the powdered bulbs of Vidary "would make an old man young again." The book contains "recipes that enable a man to retain his manhood or youthful vigour to a good old age and which generally served to make the human system invulnerable to disease and decay." When such remedies were used longevity was assured and old age banished so that a man could witness "a hundred summers in the full vigour of health, strength, and manhood." The text contained "elixirs and remedial agents which tend to improve the memory and invigorate the mental faculties as well as to increase the duration of life." There always was an overtone that rejuvenation would be accompanied by the restoration of sexual vigor.

Fig. 2

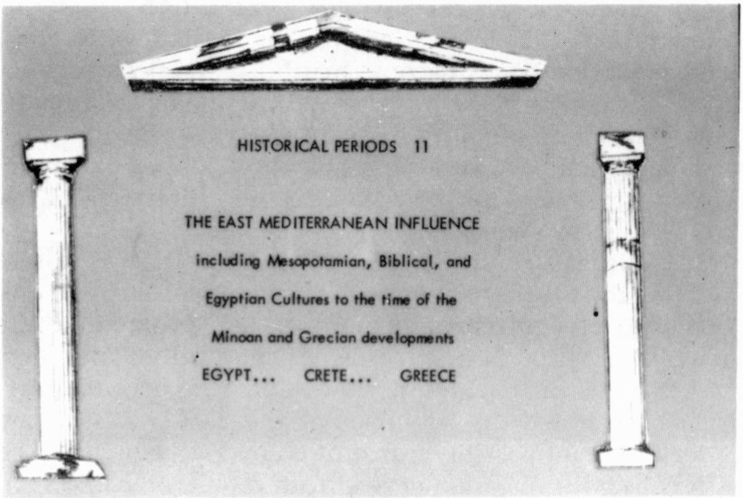

HISTORICAL PERIODS   11

THE EAST MEDITERRANEAN INFLUENCE

including Mesopotamian, Biblical, and

Egyptian Cultures to the time of the

Minoan and Grecian developments

EGYPT... CRETE... GREECE

Heading, 2nd historical section.

INFLUENCE OF THE EGYPTIAN DOCUMENTS AND THE BIBLE

The Egyptian papyrus rolls on medicine inscribed between 3000 B.C. and 1500 B.C. were said to be "the longest and the most famous of the documents relating to the more ancient practice of medicine." In the Ebers Papyrus Imhotep, Egypt's greatest physician, the Father of Medicine and spiritual predecessor of Hippocrates was called "the earliest known physician in history."[7] Osler said that he was "the first figure of a physician to stand out clearly from the mists of antiquity." He was revered successively as Asklepios, Greece's God of Medicine and as the ancestor of Aesculapius in Rome.

The Egyptians practiced the art of longevity and insured it by the routine use of emetics and sudorifics administered at specific times. As a rule, two emetics were taken each month. In column XX1, toward the end of the scroll, problems of old age were discussed under the heading of a "Book for Transforming an Old Man into a Youth."[8] Old age was stylized in the figure of an old man leaning on a cane. Detailed consideration of old age changes were known; the head of Rameses II showed tortuous calcific vessels. One papyrus concluded mournfully that "to be an old man is evil for people in every respect." The painful swelling of the heart, *uxudo,* was known to be a pathologic concomitant of aging.

From the land of Ur a religious group reached the Mediterranean and preached a profound monotheism. Ultimately they were enslaved in Egypt and put to the cruel work of building the pyramids, one of which was said to have been designed by Imhotep. Moses, a ward of the Egyptian Royal House and possibly raised as a Prince in the home of the ruler, was thought to have been trained in medicine. He was imbued with Egyptian culture. As the leader of the Israelites he led them in the Sinai desert for 40 years. Under divine guidance his philosophies were carved as the tables of the law that included the commandment to honor parents. By 850 B.C. the five books of the Bible, the Pentateuch, in which strong echoes of Egypt, Babylon, and India were evident, were completed. The collected works contained rules of hygiene extracted from tribal experience that were applied to old age. Human life was said in Genesis to have a chance of lasting 120 years but "the general attitudes throughout the Bible towards old age is one of great pessimism; it is inevitable; it is distressing ..." In the first book there is the lineage of 10 men after Adam whose lives as reckoned then were said to be 800 years. The children who mocked poor old Elisha came to disaster. In the Psalms there is a prayer of Moses, the man of God: "the days of our years are three score and ten;/Or even by strength four score years;/Yet is their pride but labor and sorrow;/For it is soon gone . . ."[9] In the 12th verse of Ecclesiastes, Koheleth, son of David (Solomon), bespoke the many infirmities of age that ended with the words "Vanity of vanities, saith the Preacher, all is vanity."

Biblical dogma ultimately formed a union with Greek thought that became an expression of the universality of man for all ages under the heading of humanism.

Fig. 3

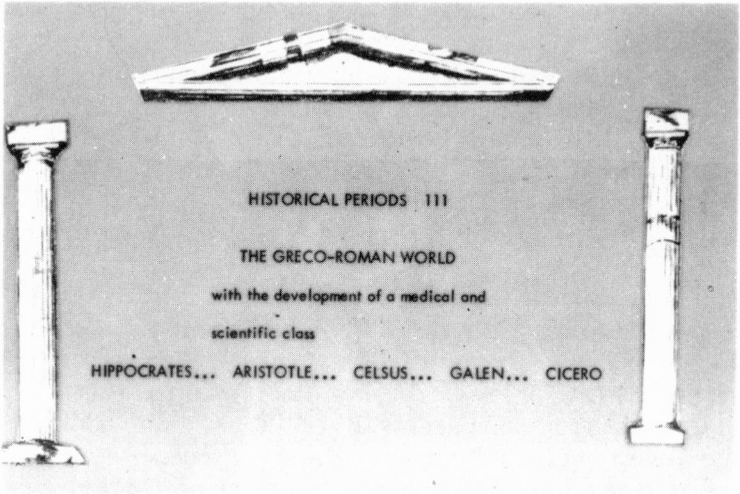

HISTORICAL PERIODS III

THE GRECO-ROMAN WORLD

with the development of a medical and

scientific class

HIPPOCRATES... ARISTOTLE... CELSUS... GALEN... CICERO

Heading, 3rd historical section.

THE GRECO-ROMAN PERIOD

The Greco-Roman period was enriched by the Hippocratic tradition and Aristotle on the Greek peninsula, and by Galen and Cicero among many notables in Rome.

The land of Greece felt the Egyptian influence, the Minoan culture of Crete and Mycenae, and all of those lines of thought that traversed land and water routes from India. The offices of the Grecian physician finally were separated from those of the priesthood. In classical Greece, youth was the prize and age a matter of distaste. Despite venerable figures such as Priam, Hecuba, and Nestor, the old were accorded little respect. Only the martial and disciplined Spartans, early seekers of the physical ideal on the Attic peninsula seemed to realize the value of their older subjects. That city-state was ruled by a gerontocratic council of 28 men 60 years of age and over elected to the gerousia. Generally "Greek writers take a very gloomy view of it, never calling it beaufitul, peaceful, or mellow, but rather dismal and oppressive."[10] There was Socrates poisoned at the age of 70, Plato who lived to 80 years of age, and Plutarch who is said to have advised his aging contemporaries to "keep your head cool and your feet warm; instead of employing medicines for every indisposition rather fast a day; and while you attend to the body, never neglect the mind."

It was in the works of Hippocrates that clinical medicine found a substantial base. This Hippocrates was said to have been the second in the hippocratic line. He taught on the island of Cos in the latter half of the 5th century B.C. The works were compiled in the 3rd or 2nd century B.C. by scholars from the Alexandrian Library as the Hippocratic Corpus. Hippocrates described a wide variety of ailments that came with aging.[11] A number of aphorisms referred to clinical considerations of the aging such as diet, fevers, illnesses, pain tolerance, constipation, and others ending in the statement that "each disease has a natural cause and nothing happens without a natural cause."

The temples of Asklepios were the Asklepieia. They were served by the Asclepiads of the guild of physicians and were centers for major clinical observations, medical training, and patient care.

Aristotle, pupil of Plato and teacher of Alexander the Great, followed the humoral theory of Empedocles and agreed that one can comprehend old age if the old body is looked upon as one that is old and dry. The Stagirite likened the diminished innate heat of old age to a feeble flame that could be extinguished readily. He expounded theories of aging and death in his book *On Youth and Old Age, On Life and Death and On Respiration.* The preservation of heat was necessary for vitality which was diminished in old age. This zealous man, who was one of Greece's most distinguished figures, had an intense curiosity about facts. His work was continued by scholars in Egypt's magnificent center of learning in Alexandria particularly in its museum when so much of the world was Hellenized and in later times when his teaching was to continue its values.

Greek influence was supplanted by the ascendancy of Rome in a rule that lasted less than a total of a thousand years divided almost equally before and after the Christian Era. Galen of Pergamon in Asia Minor who had Grecian training in medicine and wrote in that language ultimately practiced in Rome. Much of the world's material and spiritual wealth flowed through this city in which a strong family life was a household virtue that helped to protect the aging. Romans were eager to benefit by the counsel of their older leaders. The ruling body consisted of elders, the senators, in a Senate. The Romans pragmatically gave physicians a specific state role as part of the *res Romanae.* Although the function of the Roman physician was subservient to his place in the state's political organization, men like Galen were powerful influences. His views on old age were presented in his book *De Sanitate Tuenda.* Galen was preeminent in the medical world of his time and for a millenium or more to follow Celsus and Aretaeus of Cappodocia made contributions to the study of aging but it was Galen's numerous works in which most answers were sought and often thought to be found despite manifold errors. To question him then and later was to question the stability of a fixed order.

Fig. 4

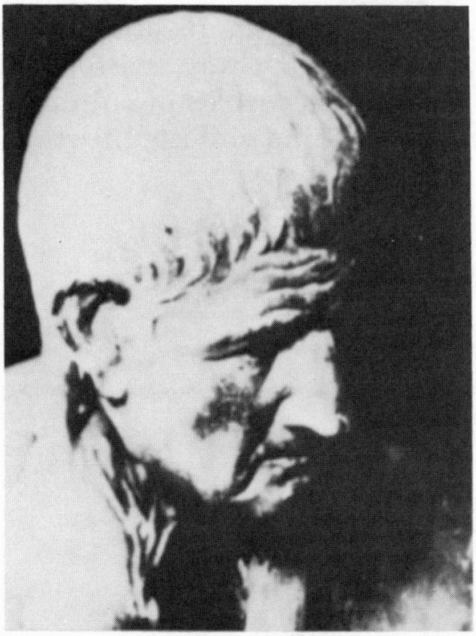

Marcus Tullius Cicero (106–43 B.C.): Cicero was of old Roman stock in whom was combined the virtues of talent as a lawyer, politician, and eloquent speaker. His book: *De Senectute, sive Cato Maior de Senectute* was printed in English by William Caxton August 12th, 1481. Franklin printed a 1744 edition in large type so that "those who begin to think on the Subject of Old Age . . . may not, in Reading, by the Pains small letters give the Eye feel the Pleasures of the Mind least allayed." The book has been a classic in the literature of aging.

Among the Roman senators Marcus Tullius Cicero wrote as a distinguished member of the Roman hierarchy and as a farmer in his sixties assuming retirement. In his book *De Senectute* he used a dialogue by Cato the Elder, the 84-year-old great republican of Rome, as the medium for his views: A stable old age is based on a stable youth. The old often are at fault for their exclusion from the company of the young because of acquired unpleasant traits. Cicero disputed the negative aspects of old age and did it with such charm that his book became one of civilization's authoritative statements. Roman virtues and qualities attained a high level in the Ciceronian writings.

As Rome declined in the 5th century the Christian Church expanded militantly. Its growth was accelerated in the 3rd century A.D. that was assisted by the depletion of Roman influences, new seats of culture, centers of nationalism, and burgeoning philosophies that were spreading through Europe.

Fig. 5

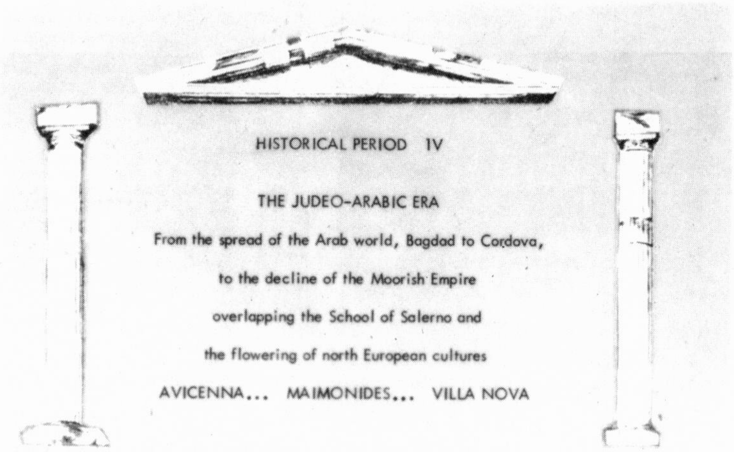

HISTORICAL PERIOD IV

THE JUDEO-ARABIC ERA

From the spread of the Arab world, Bagdad to Cordova,

to the decline of the Moorish Empire

overlapping the School of Salerno and

the flowering of north European cultures

AVICENNA... MAIMONIDES... VILLA NOVA

Heading, 4th historical section.

THE JUDEO-ARABIC PERIOD

From Baghdad to Cordova, Arab vigor spread its culture in time and space into Europe in a crescent in which one point on the west reached as far as the French city of

Tours and the one on the east as far as Vienna before receding. For about 1000 years this Byzantine-Moorish Arabic culture expanded its brand of architecture and religion. Most of its science was copied from the Greeks.[3]

Despite the surge of Arabian learning, there was one small area in which an almost undiluted Greek effort persisted. At Salerno on the Italian peninsula there was an ancient health center served originally by Greek physicians around whom a teaching center, a hospital, and a medical school developed. It was said of it apocryphally that it was founded by a Latin, an Arabian, a Greek, and a Jewish physician. Its influence lasted from its founding around 800 A.D. until Napoleon I put an end to it in 1811. Its teachings were propounded in numerous verses that were translated by Sir John Harington and were expanded to many hundreds of instructions by commentators such as Arnaldus de Villanova. No special items about old age are to be found in the salernitan writings, the so-called Flos Medicina, but Salerno was a true center of the code, teaching, and clinical methods of Hippocrates.

Meanwhile the Arabian physicians, many of whom were of the Jewish faith, were cosmopolitan, adaptable, and versed in many cultures. Among the greatest of them was Avicenna who was said to have known all of Aristotle's writings from memory. His *Canon of Medicine* followed the anatomy of Galen and the clinical observations of Hippocrates. The work of this Prince of Medicine was authoritative for 800 years.

Moses ben Maimon called Maimonides, was aristotelian in thought. He was independent in his thinking and dared to point out specific errors in Galen. Despite his lengthy and distinguished lineage he was forced to flee Cordova because of his Jewish religion and became physician to the Vizier of Saladin in Cairo. Of him it was said "he never wrote a prescription unless its efficacy was warranted by the great masters of medicine."[12] He advised older people to see physicians regularly. He favored the use of bleedings and purges. He warned old people to avoid excesses

Fig. 6

משא דרב מיימוני זצ"ל

Moses Maimonides (1135–1204): Moses ben Maimon, or Maimonides, was the scion of a distinguished Spanish family in Cordova. As a result of the persecution of the Jews, he had to flee to Fez and then to Egypt where he became physician to the Grand Vizier. He was noted as a physician, philosopher, and biblical commentator who advised the elderly to avoid excesses and to guard their health by visits to physicians at regular intervals. The universality of his thought helped to open a new era.

Fig. 7

Arnaldus de Villanova (1235–1311): This distinguished Catalan who was a physician, chemist, and diplomat contributed to the renascence of knowledge. His book *The Defense of Age and Recovery of Youth* was written toward the end of the 13th century and translated into English by Drummond in 1544. He "followed the Galenic idea that age was due to an increase in cold dry humors which could be treated with moist humors."

of all types. Cleanliness was useful for the aged as was wine. His fame was such that it was said of him that from Moses to Moses there was none greater than Moses.

His contemporary Arnaldus de Villa Nova, diplomat and physician, had "an inquiring mind, was a keen observer,

Fig. 8

¶ Here is a newe
Boke, called the defence of age
and recouery of youth transla
ted out of the famous Clarke
and ryght experte medy=
cyne Arnold de Noua
Villa very profyta=
ble for all men
to knowe.

Villanova's Monograph on Old Age: In 1544 Sir Jonas Drummond translated this work and in his introduction saluted Villanova as a "ryght experte medycyne." He must have been a very able man because he "lived to an old age."

and practical physician who, while still imbued with Arabian theory, was not afraid to set forth his own views and to defend them.[12] His book, *The Conservation of Youth and the Retardation of Aging,* was written in 1290 and because he "lived to an old age ... he must have been a very clever man." Drummond who translated the book in 1544 said that it was very profitable for all men to know its contents. The advice of the Catalan was general, based on moderation and a well-rounded existence of good hygiene.

Fig. 9

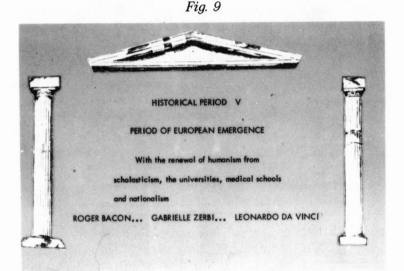

HISTORICAL PERIOD V

PERIOD OF EUROPEAN EMERGENCE

With the renewal of humanism from

scholasticism, the universities, medical schools

and nationalism

ROGER BACON... GABRIELLE ZERBI... LEONARDO DA VINCI

Heading, 5th historical section.

THE EUROPEAN EMERGENCE

This period saw the European emergence with the renewal of humanism from scholasticism, the growth of

universities, the founding of medical schools, and the out-
lines of familiar nationalism.

Friar Roger Bacon resumed the development of thought
on old age. He wrote *The Retardation of Old Age, and the
Cure of Old Age, and the Preservation of Youth* in which
he subscribed to the thought that loss of innate heat was
the cause of aging and that humans could survive at least
to 80 years of life. He looked upon the process of aging as
wholly pathologic. Although he held to the possibility of
longevity, he pointed out that the medical arts had nothing
to offer except a regimen of health by which to mitigate
aging. He was far in advance of his time when he said that
he was persuaded that if men were as careful in preserving health as they were in their efforts to recover it, they
could live longer free of disease. However, he concealed
the remedies that he thought would help to ease the effects
of aging.

Another unusual man of his time was Gabrielle Zerbi
whose work *Gerontocomia* published in Rome in 1489 was
said to be the first book expressly devoted to geriatrics. A
copy is in the Vatican Library showing Zerbi kneeling
before Pope Sixtus IV. He summarized Galenic concepts,
reviewed contributions of the Arabians, and listed 300 diseases commonly seen in the old.[13] His observations were
astute and 57 chapters were devoted to means for the
retardation of old age including clinical descriptions, a
discussion of longevity, influences of astrology, proper
sites for homes for the aged, regimens of health, and a list
of empiric remedies. He wrote in his book that "old age is
inevitable, but its end is uncertain." Only a special study
of old age could retard its maladies.

Although the major study of old age was a product of
Western culture, the subject was not neglected in other,
less-known civilizations. Cupisnique Indians who long
predated the Incas of Peru produced a remarkable portrait
of an old woman in pottery showing a wrinkled round

Fig. 10

LIS·ZERBI·VERON

Gabriele Zerbi (? 1455–1505): This Italian physician had an important career in philosophy, medicine, and medical history that began precociously at the age of 21 and ended with his assassination before he reached the age of 40. His work on aging, *Gerontocomica Scilicet de Senium Atque Victu* contained: "a very clear picture of the medical features of old age." The book was dedicated to Sixtus IV. The kneeling figure on the right is said to be that of the author.

face, toothless mouth, and quizzical expression not uncommon to those who have seen much, suffered much, and expect little.

Fig. 11

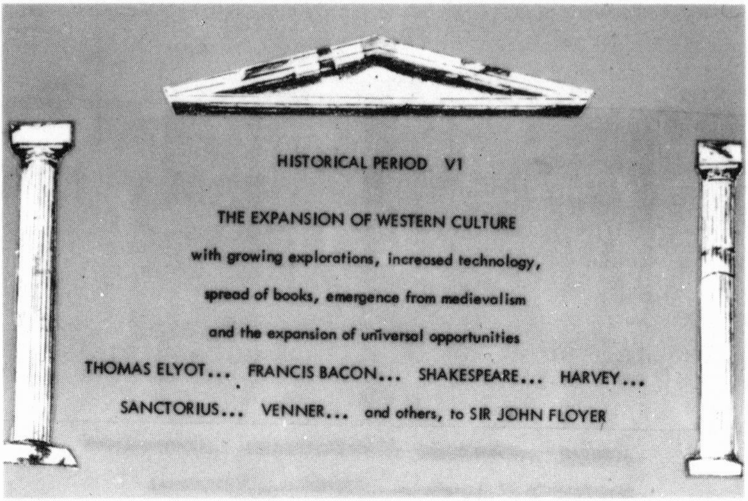

HISTORICAL PERIOD VI

THE EXPANSION OF WESTERN CULTURE

with growing explorations, increased technology,

spread of books, emergence from medievalism

and the expansion of universal opportunities

THOMAS ELYOT... FRANCIS BACON... SHAKESPEARE... HARVEY...

SANCTORIUS... VENNER... and others, to SIR JOHN FLOYER

Heading, 6th historical section.

THE RENAISSANCE

This period was one of expansion of Western culture. There were growing explorations, increased technology, the spread of books, emergence from medievalism, and an awareness of universal opportunities by mankind breaking free of class rigidity.

Much of this creative period was shown in the works of the artists Leonardo da Vinci, Lucas Cranach, Albrecht Dürer and others. The self-portrait of da Vinci with flowing white hair and beard and piercing eyes has been reproduced for 500 years as a representation of aging. In some paintings, old age appeared in all of its starkness but it is in his drawings that he outlined those features in which the aging mechanism is most apparent.

Fig. 11a

Leonardo da Vinci (1452–1519) . . . Self-portrait.

The painting of the fountain of youth, the Fons Luventutis, by Cranach the Elder is a pointed criticism of the conceits of that renascent period. Decrepit and helpless old people were carried in a variety of conveyances to enter the healing waters. After making the passage, they emerged young, gay, well-dressed, and so rejuvenated that amatory experiences were sought immediately. Cranach cast a painter's critical eye on the words of the scientists of his day with their promises of rejuvenation in which there was no dignity in aging. It is a tart criticism of those who would distort biological laws.

Marsilius Ficinus (1433–1499) was one of the bridges from the Arabs to the modern world by way of the Italian Renaissance. In his *De Triplici Vita,* he wrote of longevity in which he listed hygienic measures that have not changed much over the centuries. Cautiously, he added that an astrologer should be consulted every seven years in accordance with the theory that the body's structure changed regularly in that period of time. His most important work was his interpretation and translation of Plato.

In 1534 the famous *The Castel of Helthe* was published by Sir Thomas Elyot, a nobleman of wide interests in philosophy, education, and medicine. In his advocacy of a prudent diet he warned, "Always remember that aged men should eat often; and but little at every time, for it fareth by them as it doth by a lamp, the light whereof is almost extinct, which by pouring oil and little is kept long burning, but with much oil poured in it at once, it is put out."

This distinctive work appeared about 25 years before the influential essays and letter of Luigi Cornaro, the Apostle of Senescence. This native of Venice who lived most of what was said to be 100 years dwelled in Padua where he wrote essays of self-observation in which moderation in all things including diet, exercise, and activities were recounted to his self-satisfaction with his obvious success. His portrait by Tintoretto (?Titian) is in the Pitti Palace in

Florence and his work *La Vita Sobria, A Treatise on a Sober Life*, ranks with Cicero in its influence. More than a hundred editions followed including notable comments

Fig. 12

Luigi Cornaro (1467–1565): Luigi Cornaro's life spanned major parts of the 15th and 16th century. His poor health at age 40 led him to establish regimens of health including a diet that was restricted to 12 ounces of food and 14 ounces of fresh wine daily. At age 83, he wrote the first of 4 tracts that were published in 1558 as *Trattato de la Vita Sobria* which was influential for centuries. There were a number of translations including one by John Addison. Cornaro was called the Apostle of Senescence.

by Joseph Addison. The first of the essays was written at the age of 83 and the last when he was said to be almost 100. Benjamin Franklin in the United States commented on it in some of his many writings. Like Cicero, Cornaro became a figurehead for students of aging.

A major figure of these times was the notable Francis Bacon. This scion of a major English family who rose to heights of English power and fell in disgrace set for himself all of the realm of knowledge to explain to his fellow men. In his *History of Life and Death* there is his famous observation that "men of age object too much, consult too long, adventure too little, repent too soon, and seldom drive business home to the full period, but content themselves with a mediocrity of success." In this book there is a frontispiece showing four stages in the life of man. It was his view that "nature to be commanded must be obeyed." He was one of the most notable figures of his time who was said to be a hypochondriac who spent enough money on his medications to fill a pharmacist's shop. He devised "grains of youth" and a "Methusaleh Water." His major works were in philosophy but he believed in experiments and died from pneumonia contracted when he was studying the preservation of flesh with snow.

William Harvey, who was Bacon's physician, enters the history of aging not for his discovery of the circulation of the blood which made him first in the rank of world scientists but because he did the autopsy on Thomas Parr, that famous old rural man who was supposed to have lived 152 years. Harvey's description of the body was lucid and methodical without questioning the years claimed for the subject of the autopsy.

A prime observer of body metabolism was the famous Sanctorius, (1561–1636) professor of medicine at Padua whose major work *Ars de Statica Medicina* was published in 1614 and was authoritative throughout Europe. He was a prime observer of metabolism whose picture of himself on a large scale was duplicated repeatedly in books on

Fig. 13

Sir Francis Bacon (1561–1626): Bacon was an outstanding personality in law, philosophy, science, diplomacy, and English thought under Elizabeth I and James I. By 1597 he had produced the first of his major essays. Despite the vicissitudes of his career, he published his *Historia Vitae et Mortis* in 1623 and dedicated it: To the Present Age, and Posterity. His foresight was justified. It was his feeling that aging is "only a measure of time" and, "will not be defied."

physiology. He was a contemporary of Shakespeare, Bacon, and Harvey. He followed the humoral theory on one hand but his measurements of energy exchange including the concept of "insensible perspiration" helped to end empiricism. In aging, decay of body "spirits," he theorized, induced a "universal hardness of fibres" that led inevitably to death. The thought was not too far removed from 20th century theories of cell-inclusions causing cell errors and cellular death.

In France, the Chancellor of the University of Montpellier, Francois Ranchin, made distinguished observations of aging in his *Opuscula Medica.* In a chapter of 138 pages written in Latin, many homilies were inscribed including the bitter observation that old age homes were greenhouses wherein frail and aging plants were kept. Ranchin lived to be 81 and died of the plague when, as mayor of his city as well as a distinguished physician, he attempted to rally his community against the destructive influences of the disease.

The last important figure in gerontology for this period was Sir John Floyer, a well-known physician of Lichfield in England. He was graduated in medicine at Oxford, a friend of Samuel Johnson, and both had been touched by the King for scrofula. He had a pulmonary condition and wrote on emphysema. In his book on aging *Medicina Gerocomica* he was faithful to Galen in the subtitle which was *The Galenic Art of Preserving Old Men's Healths.* He took much from Bacon, advised moderation in all things and strongly supported his favorite recipe of hot or cold bathing according to the older person's constitution. Charcot among others looked upon this book as the first of the modern texts on geriatrics.

Others of this period require mention such as Tobias Venner who practiced in Bath and published his famous *Via Recta Ad Vitam Longam* in 1620. He was very much opposed to the use of tobacco and in favor of the use of whiskey as a remedy for old age. The aqua vitae was said to comfort a weak stomach, expel wind, dispel melancholy, preserve the humors from corruption, and protect against fainting spells. It goes directly to the heart and raises faint and feeble spirits.

One John Smith wrote a tract on aging in 1666 on the well-known verses in Ecclesiastes. In Shakespeare's works

Fig. 14

Medicina Gerocomica :

OR, THE

𝕲𝖆𝖑𝖊𝖓𝖎𝖈 𝕬𝕽𝕿

Of PRESERVING

Old Men's Healths,

EXPLAIN'D:

In Twenty CHAPTERS.

To which is added an APPENDIX, concerning the Ufe of Oyls and Unction, in the Prevention and Cure of fome Difeafes. As alfo a Method, from a *Florentine Phyfician*, of curing *Convulfions* and *Epilepfies*, by external Operation.

By Sir JOHN FLOYER, Kt. of *Lichfield*, M. D.

Pugnan lum tanquam contra morbum, fic contra Senectutem. Cicero de Senectute.

Calida lavatio & pueris & Senibus apta eft vinum dilutius pueris, Senibus meracius. Celf. de re Medi . lib. 2.

L O N D O N :

Printed for *J. Ifted*, at the *Golden-Ball*, between St *Dunftan's* Church and *Chancery Lane* End, in *Fleet-ftreet*. M DCC XXIV. Price ftitch't 2 s.

Sir John Floyer (1649–1734): The first English work on aging was written by Sir John Floyer of Lichfield, England. He studied medicine at Oxford University and ultimately was knighted in 1686. His book was called: *Medicina Gerocomica, or the Galenic Art of Preserving Old Men's Healths.* Floyer, friend of Dr. Samuel Johnson, did experimental work on respiration and made a watch with which to record pulses accurately.

there are more than 125 old people with comments on this phase of life that suggested a knowledge of the books that were available to him as well as the insights from his observations of elderly people.

Fig. 15

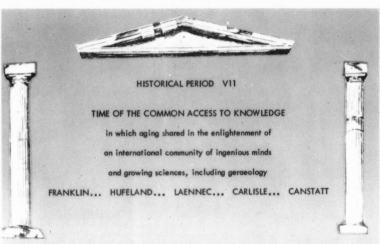

HISTORICAL PERIOD VII

TIME OF THE COMMON ACCESS TO KNOWLEDGE

in which aging shared in the enlightenment of

an international community of ingenious minds

and growing sciences, including geraeology

FRANKLIN... HUFELAND... LAENNEC... CARLISLE... CANSTATT

Heading, 7th historical section.

THE GROWTH OF COMMUNICATION AND SCIENTIFIC LEARNING

Subsequent to the period of growing awareness of the clinical knowledge of aging manifested early in the 18th century by Floyer's book, the next period of enlightening definition emerged from the growth of communications and the compounding of scientific learning.

It was during the lifetime of Benjamin Franklin (1706–1790) that the knowledge and international character of this period were personified. Franklin quoted Cheyne; published James Logan's translation of Cicero's *Cato Major* and observed a strong interest in a variety of hygienic measures by which to increase health and to deter old age. Seven years after his death, Christoph Wilhelm Hufeland in Germany published his work on macrobiosis, *The Art of Prolonging the Life of Man.* The book was sound and highly moral. It was read everywhere and was responsible for a national movement by a German population anxious to find ways to longevity. Hufeland said that the body had a "vital force" for its renewal which, when it failed, permitted aging. This friend of Goethe, and follower of Bichat and Bacon, said that "the medical art must consider every disease as an evil which cannot be too soon expelled; the macrobiotic, on the other hand, shows that many diseases may be the means of prolonging life."

One of Franklin's friends who had been his physician during his London years was John Fothergill who published *Rules for Preserving Health at all Ages* in 1762. It was Ciceronian and somewhat like Cornaro in its admonition because he advised old people to be of good mind, to seek the company of young people, and to banish the heavy spirits to which old age seems to be liable. He was an astute clinician who suspected that the heart was the seat of diseases that were manifested by explicit anginal symptoms. He brought clinical medicine to the public eye in keen observations through his understanding of epidemic diseases.

Benjamin Rush was another of the group of talented Americans with interests that were universal. He made explicit observations of the clinical diseases of old age. In the tradition of Buffon, he acknowledged the limit of mankind's lifespan. In his *Medical Inquiries and Observations* there is a chapter on the state of the body and the mind in old age with observations on its diseases and their treatment. Limited by the technology of his times, he stressed heredity, temperance, mental vigor, equanimity, and marriage as factors in longevity. It was his observation that few people die of old age; such death is the result of diseases. In his work the depth of clinical observations and insight, constrained by limitations on the knowledge of pathogenesis, was seen.

Fig. 16

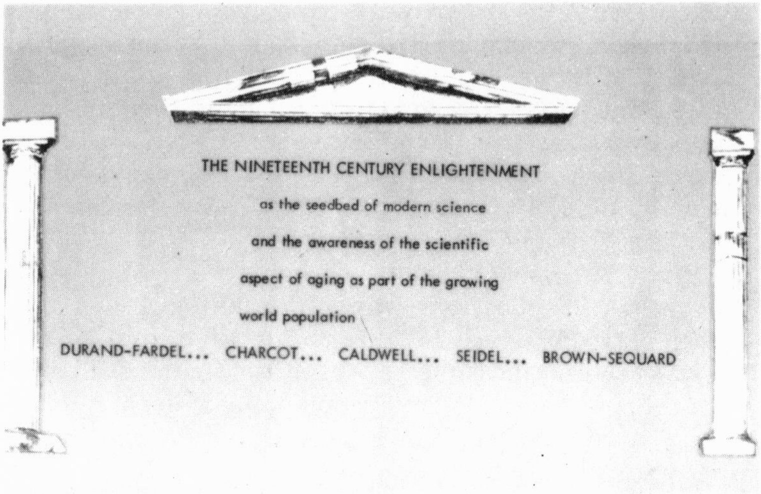

THE NINETEENTH CENTURY ENLIGHTENMENT

as the seedbed of modern science

and the awareness of the scientific

aspect of aging as part of the growing

world population

DURAND-FARDEL... CHARCOT... CALDWELL... SEIDEL... BROWN-SEQUARD

Heading, 8th historical section.

THE 19TH CENTURY

The 19th century was the premodern era in aging. In 1804, Sir John Sinclair of Edinburgh had published his four volumes in which he summarized the thoughts of much of the work on aging prior to his time and included a bibliography of 1800 publications. It was a notable achievement. His translations of classical works, his correspondence with English figures, his reviews of statistics, and his awareness of the whole field of aging capacities are outstanding.

A little over a decade later, Sir Anthony Carlisle of London, well-known surgeon and English anatomist, published his *Essay on the Disorders of Old Age* in 1817 dedicated to London's Royal College of Surgeons. He addressed himself directly to old people and advised the young to adopt a sound regimen early in life in order to secure longevity. He described diseases common to the aging and looked upon the age of 60 as the beginning of senility. His comments on surgical problems of the old were incorporated in one of the first specialty books on this subject. He pointed out that "dangerous operations are rarely adviseable in advanced age" because of the reduction in the vitality and the presence of constitutional disorders.

In Salem, Massachusetts, the famous Dr. Edward Holyoke (1728–1829) was honored on his 100th birthday having been a medical practitioner for many years. He was the teacher of Dr. James Jackson of Boston who was, "the first physician to the Massachusetts General Hospital." Holyoke used auscultation early in its development and wrote an article about it. Centenarian physicians are an uncommon phenomenon.

A generation after Sinclair, Carl Canstatt in Germany published a work on geriatrics that was described as the best that ever had been written on the subject. It was a thorough aggregation of all of the facts logically considered that could contribute to the knowledge of old age. He theorized that death of individual cells represented general molecular death that could not be replaced. This work published in 1839 duplicated in content by Prus of France in the following year was written by a man whose own life lasted but 43 years.

Meanwhile many works flourished including those by Day and others but even as late as 1863 Daniel Maclachlan (1807–1870) of England wrote that there was little in English literature on old age that contained valuable information on the hygiene and diseases except for some minor efforts. Only four years later Jean-Martin Charcot began his lectures on diseases of the aged at La Salpêtrière in Paris. He was a master clinician with far ranging insights and a sense of drama. He had learned that certain diseases in the old have a long period of latency with the formation ultimately of pathologic conditions. In his clinical lectures on diseases of old age published in 1867 with dignity he expounded: "The course which we today inaugurate is proposed to acquaint you with the general characteristics that distinguish the pathology of old age from that of adult life and to fix your attention on some of those diseases which are more especially met with in hospitals for the aged." The book was translated into English by Leigh H. Hunt, supplemented importantly by Dr. A. L. Loomis of New York in 1881. With it the field had found its measuring stick. By the time of August Seidel's monograph of old age in the next decade, the modern era was apparent. In 1896 Dr. C. A. Stephens created a laboratory for the study of old age in Maine and started a magazine called *Long Life.*

Fig. 17

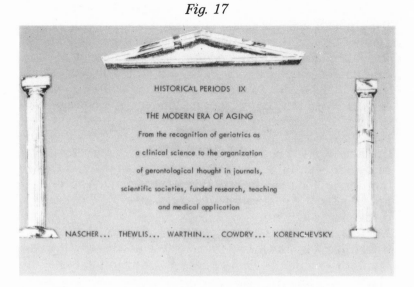

Heading, 9th historical section.

THE MODERN ERA

In the 20th century, Elie Metchnikoff (1845–1916) introduced his concept of autointoxication as the detrimental effects that were assumed to be the result of the absorption of toxins from intestinal bacteria, and received the Nobel Prize in 1908 for his many contributions to biology and the study of aging. In spite of all that had been documented, Charles Sedgwick Minot (1852–1914) of West Roxbury, Massachusetts said that "From the time of Cicero to the time of Holmes, numerous authors have written on old age, yet among them all we shall scarcely find any one who had title to be considered a scientific writer upon the subject." This statement was too general. It was written just about the time that Nascher had coined the word *geriatrics,* who saw the inclusion of a section on the subject in a major clinical journal, lectured in two medical schools, and ultimately was named honorary president of the American Geriatrics Society. By the time of his death at age 81 in 1944, this science was on its way. He, like 19th century William Thoms, helped to clear out some of the fancies that long had restricted the development of the subject. It was Thoms, deputy librarian of the House of Lords who published his work *Longevity in Man: Its Facts and Fiction* in 1873 in which he questioned the validity of the story of Thomas Parr's claimed longevity. Nascher in his way set the dogma for the uniqueness of the clinical problems of aging.

William Osler, called the greatest physician of his times, was an American Charcot who never gave up his Canadian citizenship. As he was leaving the United States to take on the Regius Professorship of Medicine at Oxford he referred to Trollope's novel *The Fixed Period* with some lighthearted comments to the effect that most achievements in life are attained before the age of 40 and that by 60 so little could be anticipated that the elderly might as well be chloroformed. The statement that "Dr. Osler says all men over 60 should be killed" caused headlines in the world's press and the name of this noted teacher was marred in the public mind.

Warthin, Minot, Child,[14] and others advanced the subject of the science of aging. In 1924 G. Stanley Hall wrote his outstanding book *Senescence* and four years later Miles[12] at Stanford University turned the minds of a number of important scientists to the subject of old age. Within five years Edmund Vincent Cowdry followed his studies of arteriosclerosis with the publication of *The Problems of Ageing* and the modern era had its text. The journals, the societies, the international group so well served by V. Korenchevsky of the Nuffield Foundation at Oxford and the involvement of private foundations as well as national resources in all aspects of aging are the ongoing aspects of a history of a subject traced to the lives of men from the static civilizations of the Far East to the dynamism of the West in which at this point all nations participate. With the Congress on Aging in Kiev in 1938 and the formation of the International Association of Gerontology at Liège in 1950, studies of aging were applied effectively to all human spheres.

In retrospect, the general review of the arbitrary periods of aging's scientific history had to omit the names and works of many distinguished figures. The omissions became more apparent with the gerontologic orientation that was intensified in the latter part of the nineteenth century.

Three major currents of thought have characterized works on old age over the centuries. The views and experiences of perceptive individuals like Cicero and Cornaro who shared their personal observations are typical of the first era from the beginning of literate history to the 17th century. The second period owes a debt to clinical observations of the hippocratic type that took definite shape in the 19th century when the unique nature of illness in the aging body was described by major clinicians such as Durand-Fardel and Charcot. The third or physiologic movement that was initiated by Sanctorius was carried forward by Quetelet and Jonathan Hutchinson. It continues with evaluations of metabolism in which age is a standard variable. At present a growing technology holds the promise of altering genetic codes and changing the nature, rate of progression, and effects of those pathologic processes that mature and become evident in the old body.

Biologists in gerontology are committed to the ways of longevity. In the acceptance of this responsibility, they are obliged to seek ways to overcome associated pathologic states. Eos forgot to seek immortal youth in her husband when she asked Zeus for an eternal god-like life for him; the fate of Tithonus as a dry old cricket chirping endlessly is a reminder that longevity without well-being is a price too high to pay for survival.

The physician in geriatrics has a different set of responsibilities, namely, an obligation to use the most effective diagnostic and therapeutic measures that are available for aging patients within a receptive social form. This type of longevity is the product of improved clinical values. History's commitment to gerontology and geriatrics is to create awareness of the biologic and clinical legacies.

NOTES

1. Hamilton E: The Greek Way. New York, WW Norton, 1942

2. Freeman JT: The sociologic aspects of aging: gerocomy. *W Va Med J* 50:1–12, 1954

3. Mettler CC: History of Medicine (ed FA Mettler). Philadelphia, Blakiston, 1947

4. Martí-Ibanez F: The Epic of Medicine. New York, CN Potter, 1967

5. Huang Ti Nei Ching Su Wên, The Yellow Emperor's Classic of Internal Medicine (trans Iveith I) Baltimore, Williams & Wilkins, 1949

6. The Sushruta Samhita (Engl trans KK Bhishgratna) Calcutta, Publ by author, 1907

7. The Edwin Smith Surgical Papyrus (trans JH Breasted) Chicago, Univ Chicago Press, 1930

8. Grant RL: Concepts of aging: an historical review. *Persp Biol & Med* 6:443–478, 1963

9. Psalms Book IV, 90:10

10. Hall GS: Senescence, the last Half of Life. New York, D Appleton, 1923

11. The Genuine Works of Hippocrates (trans F Adams) New York, William Wood & Co, 1929

12. Freeman JT, Webber IL: Perspectives in Aging. *Gerontologist* 5, Pt 2: I–IX & 1–53, 1965

13. Zeman FD: Life's Later Years. Studies in the medical history of old age Pt 8 The revival of learning. *J Mt Sinai Hosp* 12 833–846, 1945

14. Child CM: Senescence and Rejuvenescence. Chicago, Univ Chicago Press, 1915

2

100 Distinguished Works on Aging, Old Age, and the Aged

By chance, choice, or both, 100 is a number that seems to have taken on special meaning for some students of aging. At this notable point in living for the few that attain that age, the pathologic and attritional aspects of senescence are put aside by testimonies to the capacity for survival and by traditional requests for advice that usually are received dimly, answered vaguely, quoted verbatim, and read with skepticism.

Interest in the very old is stimulated periodically by the discovery of ancient individuals and by accounts of long-living groups in Afghanistan, Abkhasia, Ecuador, and elsewhere.[1] Colombia dedicated a stamp to one Javier Pereira, 167 years of age. His advice for longevity took the form of a salute to his country's economy. He is quoted on the stamp as having said that he owed his long life to the fact that he smoked good cigars, drank much fine coffee, and did not worry. The U.S.S.R. matched this philatelic memoriam with a stamp to celebrate the 148th birthday of Makhmud Aivazov, a farmer from Azerbeijan, presumably a representative of the traditional long life of citizens in some regions of his country.[2] Other very old people have had their daily activities and birthday statements documented in the same way as was done for the 17th century England's 152-year-old Thomas Parr during his lifetime.

In the 18th century, James Easton published a list of names of 1712 long-lived people from 6 A.D. to 1799 and enlargened some of his citations with descriptive notes. Acceptances into his files were not very critical. Late in the 19th century, doubting William J. Thoms, Deputy Librarian to the English House of Lords, penned an agnostic tale to many of these stories and introduced a most welcome note of question to the history of many presumptive, and unchallenged, accounts of centenarians.

The literature contains all types of examples of aging, old age, and the aged. The 4,600 year old life of an Arizona bristle cone, once cited as the oldest living thing, is second to claims for a 6,000 year old living tree in China. The satyric old lion, Frasier, had the account of his lengthy leonine life, embellished as it was by his ability to impregnate a number of young lionesses, placed in an encyclopedia.

Works on old age achieve distinction in the literature for their priority, for their enduring influence, their pioneer place in human ideas, and even by the chance of discovery. One hundred distinguished works on the subject share the same enthusiasm for such special markers as those that are used to designate a new year, a birthdate, a holiday, and similar measures by which mortality's finiteness temporarily is obscured. Even the centenary of the American Medical Association spurred the study of the lifespan of United States physicians.[3]

The ability to identify, obtain, read, and judge the thousands of works on old age that make up a total bibliography of the subject is beyond practical attainment. In 1804, Sir John Sinclair of Edinburgh said that there are "about two thousand works of different sizes, connected with gen-

Fig. 18

THE

CODE

OF

HEALTH AND LONGEVITY;

OR,

A CONCISE VIEW

OF THE PRINCIPLES

CALCULATED FOR

THE PRESERVATION OF HEALTH,

AND

THE ATTAINMENT OF LONG LIFE.

BEING AN ATTEMPT TO PROVE THE PRACTICABILITY OF CONDENS-
ING, WITHIN A NARROW COMPASS, THE MOST MATERIAL
INFORMATION HITHERTO ACCUMULATED, REGARD-
ING THE MOST USEFUL ARTS AND SCIENCES, OR
ANY PARTICULAR BRANCH THEREOF.

BY

SIR JOHN SINCLAIR, BART,

VOL. I.

THE SECOND EDITION.

Neque enim ulla alia re homines propius ad Deos accedunt, quam salutem
hominibus dando.—CICERO, PRO LIGARIO, C. 38.

EDINBURGH:

PRINTED FOR ARCH. CONSTABLE & CO.; AND T. CADELL AND
W. DAVIES, AND J. MURRAY, LONDON.

1807.

Sir John Sinclair (1754–1835): Sir John Sinclair was born of a titled family in Scotland. He came to the English bar in 1782 and later served energetically as a member of Parliament. Among his various commitments, he was interested in and introduced the word Statistics. He wrote extensively on a number of subjects and was called: "the most indefatigable man in Britain."

His *Code of Health* published in Edinburgh in 1807 took a long time to achieve the recognition in the field of aging that it deserved. Sinclair's bibliography is in these four volumes and contained almost 2,000 references to works on aging.

eral inquiries regarding health and longevity, all of which ought to be considered with the greatest care...." This quotation was taken from his *The Code of Health and Longevity* that had a second edition in 1807. His choices did not have the precise descriptions that modern bibliographies require.

The likelihood of omitting a major work from a selective list rises in proportion to the task but is protected to some extent by the tendency among historians to repeat citations. A statement by Bostwick[4] in 1851 is a bulwark against adverse critics and shields entrepreneurs who have the temerity to act so authoritatively, if any defense of an honest effort is needed.

> Everything of a metaphysical or speculative character has been carefully avoided, so that whosoever may feel disposed to raise objections, must do so not in accordance with any whim, prejudice or superstition which may afflict him, but by denying either the truth of the premises, or the legitimacy of the deductions.

Those who wish to raise objections must get past the Bostwickian wicket.

In order to prepare the list, titles were taken from a personal collection of an unpublished bibliography of gerontology. Initial selections were compared with works that were included in the publications of major historians in gerontology. When a majority of these writers included a title that was in agreement, the work was considered to be endorsed by consensus, and was placed in this list. The remainder that were included depended on the chance of turning up an overlooked masterpiece, or by fluctuations in the scale of values, and even by haphazard inclusions (or exclusions) common to such projects. One example is Ranchin's *Opuscula Medica* published in 1641. In this work by the Chancellor of the University of Montpellier

Medical School, a fine chapter on aging was found by chance in a book that came to auction. The discovery led to a biography of Francois Ranchin as a pioneer writer in geriatrics.[5] When the bibliography of publications by other authors turned up a name or work that was unknown or had been bypassed accidentally, it was weighed for its appropriate place in the final selections.

The choice of a fixed number of titles carries with it a degree of bias that, like altruism, is a most human of traits. In the last resort, the difficulty was not to find suitable material for acceptance, but to limit selections arbitrarily to the chosen number with reasonable objectivity.

The lay and scientific literature contain many excellent works on aging that reflect a regular but questionable tendency of many historians to accept the validity of scholarly predecessors with an uncritical eye. Titles in the present list probably would cause little dissent among authorities. Most could be accepted by gerontology scholars who would sanction variations as acceptable expressions of a personal choice. A typical example is the work of Durand-Fardel published in 1854. For the medical world, his book was far superior as a study of geriatrics than the initial publication by Charcot in 1867 that needed the additional chapters by the American, A. L. Loomis in 1881 to enhance its value. Charcot's work took precedence over his earlier colleague because of the immense influence he exerted on the subject derived from his eminence in medicine. (As an answer to this reflection, both works have been included.)

Arguments could ensue over the relative merits of omitted titles. Why should one book be selected in preference to other equal competitors? The selected author's general distinction may give emphasis to his views on old age that are only part of his full canon and he gains this endorsement by association. The tendency of bibliographers to repeat the errors of their mentors makes for a tight circle that is difficult to break, just as portraits of some men are

Fig. 19

Jean-Martin Charcot (1825–1893): The notable aspects of the life of the
great French neurologist, Charcot, are labeled by his many eponyms. In
1867 he began his lectures on aging at La Salpêtrière which was the site
of most of his clinical observations. This gifted man published a text:
*Lécons Cliniques sur les Maladies des Vieillards et les Maladies Chron-
iques* in 1868. The chapters were translated by Hunt in 1881 and rounded
out by perceptive chapters by A. L. Loomis, a New York clinician famous
in his own right. Such was the force of Charcot's personality and reputa-
tion that the book dominated the field of aging for decades.

selected to hang in halls while peer colleagues (who may
have been better) lacked some quality, or support, that
tilted the selection. Such eclecticism does not stand up to

critical investigation, and possibly this is true of some items on this list.

In the gerontologic literature there have been many references to the historical bibliography of old age. Nascher in his 1914 text and his student Thewlis in his book published in 1919, both had prefatorial narratives about the classical items in the field. The works of Sinclair, von Haller, Ploucquet, Choulant,[6] Mueller-Deham and Rabson (1942) and others contained major bibliographies. Bibliographic lists such as the Osler *Bibliotheca*[7] were reviewed personally for titles. The search required some a priori knowledge of what should be included in 100 selections as part of an ultimate comprehensive bibliography.

As a feature of its first Graduate Fortnightly 1928, the New York Academy of Medicine held an interesting exhibit consisting of alchemical books, books on old age listed chronologically from 1544 to 1925, titles on old age in poetry and lay prose followed by illustrations of old age. The noteworthy exhibit consisted of 159 items.[8]

In 1938, a history of geriatrics was published in the *Annals of Medical History*[9] in the same year as Kiev's Congress on Aging. The Congress proceedings published in 1940 included a notable bibliography of more than 1000 titles.[10] Important references were found in the first volume of the Surgeon-General's Library of 1879. In Cowdry's *Problems of Ageing* (2nd ed. 1942) McCay had a chapter with a number of historical quotations.[11] Subsequently there was an out-pouring of many fine historical works notably by Zeman, Burstein, Gruman, Grmek, Lüth, Grant, Howell, Nikitin, Steudel, and Vischer, and others much of which was summarized in the *Perspectives of Aging* published in 1963.[12]

At the 8th Congress of the International Association of Gerontology in Washington, D.C. in 1969, the exhibits included one of historical books on old age. Subsequently, professional booksellers became more aware of the demand for such material and began to identify titles by specific headings in their catalogues. The card catalogues of a number of libraries in Canada, United States, Italy, France, England, Scotland, Ireland, Hungary, Austria, Turkey, and Germany have been reviewed personally and by mail. As far as possible, copies of their card files have been obtained and placed in a master file. As might be expected, many catalogues contain the same titles that confirms the conclusion that a collection by almost any bibliographer in the field will be similar except for differences in emphasis or personal inclination.

In honor of hundreds of workers and titles that were passed over inadvertently or arbitrarily to meet the limits of the project an additional 20 titles were added. The appended titles are an expression of a measure of regret and a tithe of recognition for the exclusions. Why not include Trollope for his *Fixed Period* that surfaced in a press storm when quoted by Osler who was getting ready to leave Johns Hopkins for Oxford? Charles Willson Peale for his letter to Jefferson,[13] Polonius for his advice to Laertes, Bogomolets[14] for his pioneer thoughts, Mueller-Deham for his splendid clinical text translated one year before the fine book of Stieglitz that was published in 1943, and others are notable works that belong in a major bibliography.

The scientific aspects of old age have been recorded from earliest times in parallel with social progress. The degree of social and medical competency can be judged by the total fraction of the human capacity for longevity that is attained by an increasing number of people who have a normal birth. Even when the environment was not so favorable, i.e., plagued by disease, nutritional problems, wars, high infant mortality (it took the birth of approximately 9 children in Elizabethan England to produce one to two long-living persons), there were long survivors whose senectitude attracted the attention of scientists, artists, and other authorities.

In order to reflect the social wisdom that such aging attracted, some of the outstanding works of these authors have been included not only for their scientific value but as a reflection of man's understanding of aging.

REFERENCES

1. Leaf A: Everyday is a gift when you are over 100. *Nat Geographic Mag* 143:93, 1973

2. Freeman JT, Shore H: Gerontophilately. Private Publ, Dallas, Texas Vol 1 No 1, 1976

3. Dublin LI, Spiegleman M: The longevity and mortality of American physicians. 1938–1942. *JAMA* 134:1211, 1947

4. Bostwick H: An Inquiry into the Cause of Natural Death. New York, Stringer & Townsend, 1851

5. Freeman JT: Francois Ranchin Contributor of an early chapter in geriatrics. *J Hist Med & Allied Sc,* 4:422, 1950

6. Choulant JL: Handbuch der Bückerkunde fur die Altere Medicin. Leipzig, L Voss, 1828

7. Osler W: Bibliotheca ... Osleriana; a Catalogue of Books Illustrating the History of Medicine and Science. Oxford, Clarendon Press, 1929

8. Catalogue of an exhibition of books, etc., on old age, held in the Library of the New York Academy of Medicine in connection with the first annual Graduate Fortnightly, October, 1928-*Bull NY Acad Med* 5:119, 1929

9. Freeman JT: The history of geriatrics. *Ann Med Hist* 10:324, 1938

10. "———": Kiev to Kiev in Gerontology: 1938–1972. *Gerontologist* 13:403, 1973

11. McCay CM: Down through the ages. Chap 34:908, in Cowdry, EV: Problems of Ageing, Baltimore, Williams & Wilkins, (2nd ed), 1942

12. Freeman JT, Webber IL: Perspectives in Aging (suppl) *Gerontologist* 5:1, 1965

13. Peale CW: An Epistle to a Friend on the Means of Preserving Health, Promoting Happiness and Prolonging the Life of Man to its Natural Period. Philadelphia, R Aitken, 1803

14. Bogomolets A: Problèmes de la Médécine Expérimentale dans la Lutte Contre le Vieillessement Prémature L'Organisme. CTAPOCTb, Kiev, Academy of Sciences, Ukraine SSR, 1939–1940, chap 1

Alberti, Michael (1682–1757) Tractatio medica de longaevitate hominis, naturalibus nonnullis mediis adjuvanda et promovenda, regulis praecipue diaeteticis accommodata, simplici ac vitae animali optime quadrante modo commendata a . . . Halae Magdeb., Apud J. C. Hendelium, 1732

Albertus Magnus (Albert von Bollstädt) (?1193–1280) De juventute et senectute, morte et vita. Codd. sunt in Bodley. n. 1320

Alpini, Prosperi (1553–1617) De praesagienda vita et aegrotantium septem; in quibus ars tota hippocratica praedicendi in aegrotis varios morborum eventus, quum ex veterum medicorum dogmatis, tum ex longa accurataque observatione, nova methodo elucescit. Cum praefatione Hermanni Boerhaave. Lugduni Bat., I. Severirii, 1710

Amicus, Diomedes (fl. 16th c.) De morbis sporadibus opus novum . . . in quo singulari cum facilitate, exactoque cum iudicio ea omnia, que ad illarum corporis humani affectionum diagnosticen, prognosticen, therapeuticen, prophylacticen, analepticen: item ad gerocomicen: denique ad tria medica instrumenta in universum pertinent, plenissimè explicantur. Venetiis, J. A. and J. de Franciscis, 1605

Anselmus, Aurelius (ca. 17th c., fl. 1605) Gerocomica, sive de senum regimine, opus non modo philosophis & medicis gratum, sed omnibus hominibus utile, Venetiis: Apud F. Ciottum, 1606

Aristotle, (384–322 B.C.) Parva naturalia: a) De sensu et sensato, de memoria et reminiscentia, de somno et vigilia, de longitudine et brevitate vitae. b) De iuventute et senectute, de inspiratione et respiratione, de vita et morte, de motu animalium, de motu cordis. c) De bona fortuna, de causis. Padua, anon. pr., 1473

Armstrong, John (1709–1779) The art of preserving health: A poem. London, A. Millar, 1744

Arnaldus de Villanova (1235?–1311) Liber de conservanda iuventute et retardanda senectute. Liber de conferentibus et nocentibus principalibus membris nostri corporis. Lipsiae, Wolfgang Monacensis, 1511. See also, De conservatione juventutis et retardatione senectutis. (The conservation of youth and defense of age) 1290 A.D. (trans. Dr. Jonas Drummond 1544)

Aschoff, Ludwig (1866–1942) Zur normalen und pathologischen Anatomie des Greisenalters. Urban & Schwartzenberg, Berlin & Wien, 1938

Bacon, Francis, Vicecomitis S. Albani, Baronis de Verulamio (1561–1626) Historia vitae et mortis; sive, titulus secundus in historia naturali et experimentalis ad condendam philosophiam, quae est Instaurationis Magnae, pars tertia. London, In officina I. Haviland, impensis M. Lownes, 1623

Bacon, Roger (1214?–1294) De retardandis senectutis accidentibus, et de sensibus conservandis. Transcribed by Benedictus Hermanus de Bubach, Feb. 14, 1473; or the first English edition: The cure of old age, and preservation of youth, shewing how to cure and keep off the accidents of old age; and how to preserve the youth, strength, and beauty of body, and the senses and all the faculties of both body and mind. Translated out of Latin, with annotations and an account of his life and writings, by Richard Browne. London, Printed for Tho. Flesher at the Angel and Crown, and Edward Evets at the Green Dragon, 1683

Balfour, George William (1823–1903) The senile heart; its symptoms, sequelae and treatment. London, A. and C. Black, 1894. Based on, The senile heart. Edinb med J., 1886–1887 32:769–778; 1887–1888, 33:681–688

Beard, George M. (1839–1883) Legal responsibility in old age, based on researches into the relation of age to work. Read before the Medico-Legal Society of the City of New York, March, 1873. Republished with notes and additions from the transactions of the Society. New York, Russells' Printing House, 1874

Bible: Ecclesiastes XII,1–8; Psalms XC, 10; Genesis V, 19 and VI, 1 for the longevity of many figures; rules of hygiene; Leviticus XI–XV; commandment to honor elders, Deuteronomy V, 6–18; response of Barzillai the Gileadite to King David; Second Samuel XIX, 32; David and Abishag 1st Kings I

Fig. 20

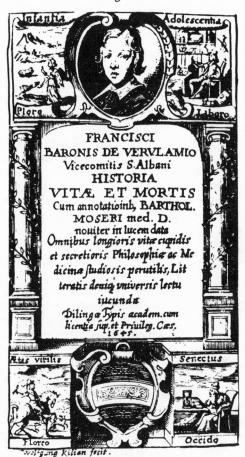

Title page of Sir Francis Bacon's work on aging, *Historia Vitae e Mortis,* 1645 edition

Bichat, Marie-Francois Xavier (1771–1802) Récherches physiologiques sur la vie et la mort. Paris, Chez Brosson, Gabon et Cie (1800) an VIII

Boerhaave, Hermanno von (1668–1738) Aphorismi de cognoscendis et curandis morbis. Leyden: J. Vander Linden. 1709, translated, Aphorisms: Concerning the knowledge and cure of diseases. Translated from the last edition printed in Latin at Leyden, 1715. With useful observations and explanations by J. Delacoste. London, W. & J. Annes, 1724

Brisienus, Hieronymous (fl. ca. 1590), or, Brisienus (Brescinna) Girolamo, Geraeologia. Tridanti, 1585

Brown-Séquard, Charles Edouard (1817–1894) Des effets produits, chez l'homme par des injections sous-cutanées d'un liquide retiré des testicules frais de cobaye et de chien. Compt Rend Soc Biol 41:415–422, 1889

Buffon, M. le Comte, Georges Louis Leclerc (1707–1780) Oeuvres complètes. Tome quatrième, Histoire Naturelle de l'homme. Histoire naturelle de l'homme, de la vieillesse et de la mort. Paris, De L'imprimerie Royale, 1774, pp 336–520

Caldwell, Charles (1772–1853) Thoughts on the effects of age on the human constitution. A special introductory. Louisville, J. C. Noble, 1846

Canstatt, Carl Friedrich (1807–1850) Die Krankheiten des höheren Alters and ihre Heilung. Erlängen, Ferdinand Enke, 1839

Cardani, Hieronymi (1501–1576) Mediolensis philosophi ac medici celeberrimi operum. Tomus secundus quo continentur moralia quaedam et physica. 1 De utilitate ex adversis capienda, Liber II, Senectute pp 50–52; III Theonoston, Liber II, seu de vita producenda atque in columitate corporis conservanda, pp 372–402; Tomus sextus qui est medicinalium primus. De Sanitate Tuenda, Liber IV, De Senectute pp 242–294

Carlisle, Sir Anthony (1768–1840) An essay on the disorders of old age, and on the means for prolonging human life. London, Longman, Hurst, Rees, Orme, and Brown, 1817

Charcot, Jean-Martin (1825–1893) Lécons cliniques sur les maladies des vieillards et les maladies chroniques. Paris, A. Delahaye, 1867, after his paper, Maladies chroniques: maladies des vieillards. Gaz. d. hôp. Paris, 1866 XXXIX; 257; 273; 293. *Also in,* Med Times & Gaz, London, 1867, 1:245; 463 subsequently translated into English, Clinical lectures on the diseases of old age. Trans. by Leigh H. Hunt, with additional lectures by Alfred L. Loomis, New York, W. Wood & Co., 1881

Cheyne, George (1681–1743) An essay on health and long life. London, G. Strahan, 1724

Fig. 21

LEÇONS CLINIQUES

SUR LES

MALADIES DES VIEILLARDS

ET LES

MALADIES CHRONIQUES

PAR

J.-M. CHARCOT

Agrégé à la Faculté de médecine de Paris, Médecin de l'hospice
de la Salpêtrière

RECUEILLIES ET PUBLIÉES PAR

B. BALL

Agrégé à la Faculté de médecine de Paris

———

PREMIER FASCICULE.

(Avec figures dans le texte.)

I. CARACTÈRES GÉNÉRAUX DE LA PATHOLOGIE SÉNILE.
II. DE L'ÉTAT FÉBRILE CHEZ LES VIEILLARDS.

⚜

PARIS

ADRIEN DELAHAYE, LIBRAIRE-ÉDITEUR

PLACE DE L'ÉCOLE-DE-MÉDECINE

—
1867

Léçons Cliniques sur les Maladies des Vieillards et les Maladies Chroniques. The title page of the second edition of Charcot's work on aging was revised and published in Paris in 1874. The first edition of 1867 contained the lectures given in the previous year.

Cicero, Marcus Tullius (106–43 B.C.) De senectute, sive Cato major de senectute. English, Westminster, William Caxton, 12 August 1481

Cohausen, Joannes Henricus (1665–1750) Hermippus redivivus, sive exercitatio physico-medica curiosa de methodo rara ad CXV annos prorogandae senectutis per anhelitum puellarum, ex veteri monumento Romano deprompta, nunc artis medicae

Fig. 22

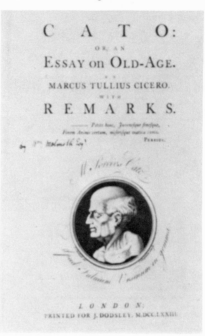

Cato Maior: In 1744 Benjamin Franklin published an edition of Cicero's classical work that was translated into English by Mr. James Logan of Philadelphia.

    fundamentis stabilita, et rationibus atque exemplis, nec non singulari chymiae philosophicae paradoxo illustrata et confirmata. Francofurti ad Moenum, J.B. Andrea & H. Hort, 1742

Cornaro, Luigi (1467–1566) Trattato de la vita sobria. Padova, Gratioso Perchacina, 1558

Cowdry, E. Vincent (1888–1975) Problems of ageing; biological and medical aspects. Josiah Macy, Jr. Foundation publication edited by Dr. Cowdry. Baltimore, Williams & Wilkins, 1939

Cranach, Lucas the Elder (1472–1553) Composition of the picture, Fons Juventutis, executed by his son, Lucas (1515–1586) in 1546

Cusa, Nicholas de, Cardinal Cusanus also known as, Nikolas Krebs of Cues (1401–1464) Opera omnia. De staticis experimentis of Nicolaus Cusanus. Ann M Hist, 4:115–135, 1922 (H. Viets)

Fig. 23

TRATTATO

DE LA VITA SOBRIA

DEL MAGNIFICO M.

LVIGI CORNARO

N O B I L E

VINITIANO.

In Padoua, appreſſo Gratioſo Perchacino

M D LVIII.

Trattato de la Vita Sobria: This work of four parts was published by
Luigi Cornaro in 1558.

da Vinci, Leonardo (1452–1519) Portraits of aging men, anatomi-
cal sketches of old subjects, and the painting of himself in his
later years.

de Bacquere, Benedictus (1613–1678) Senum medicus, quaedam praescribens observanda, ut sine magnis molestiis aliquousque senectus protrahatur. Opus rarum ac curiosum, omnibus longam vitam producere cupientibus utile, or, Senum salvator, salutaria suggerens media, per quae quis de senectute bona transeat in juventutem perpetuam. Coloniae Agrippinae, Joa. Widenfeldt, 1673

de Moivre, Abraham (1667–1754) Annuities upon lives, or the valuation of annuities upon any number of lives: As also of reversions. With Appendix concerning the expectations of life, and the probabilities of survivorship. Dublin, 1st ed., 1724; 2nd ed., corrected, S. Fuller, 1731

de Pomis, David (1525–1593) Enarratio brevis, de senum affectibus praecavendis, atque curandis rationali methodo decorata, aeque atque praestantissimis, arcanis que auxiliis, in quibusdam profligandis morbis, insignita. Venetiis, I. Variscum, 1558

Durand-Fardel, M. (1815–1899) Traité clinique et pratique des maladies des vieillards. Paris, G. Baillière, 1854

Easton, James (1722–1799) Human longevity; recording the name, age, place of residence, and year of the decease of 1,712 persons who attained a century and upwards from A.D. 66 to 1799, comprising a period of 1,733 years. With anecdotes of the most remarkable. Salisbury, Printed and sold by J. Easton, 1799

Ficinus, Marsilius (1433–1499) De triplici vita aurea volumina tria, videlicet. Primus, de vita sana; seu, de cura valetudinis eorum: qui litterarum studio incumbunt. Secundus, de vita longa. Tertius, de vita celitus comparanda. Item apologia quedam; in qua de medicina; astrologia; vita mundi subtiliter tractatur. Item de magis: qui Christum statim natum adoraverunt. Item quod ad vitam securitas & animi tranquillitas necessaria sit. Item brevis annotatio. Novissime post omnes impressiones ... recognita & erroribus expurgata. Florentiae, A. Mischominus, 3 December 1489

Fischer, Joa. Bernard (1685–1772) De senio, eiusque gradibus et morbis, nec non de eiusdem acquisitione tractatus. Recensio historica primi senii, grandaevitatis et longaevitatis. De morbis senilibus, eorumque curatione. De methodo salvam longaevitatem acquirendi. Praemissa praefatione Andreae Eliae Büchneri. Erfordiae, Joa. Frider. Weber, 1754

Flourens, Marie-Jean Pierre (1794–1867) De la longevité humaine et de la quantité de vie sur le globe. Paris, Garnier, 1854

Floyer, Sir John (1649–1734) Medicina gerocomica: or, The Galenic art of preserving old men's healths, explain'd: in twenty chapters. To which is added an appendix, concerning the use of oyls and unction, in the prevention and cure of some diseases. As also a method, from a Florentine physician, of curing convulsions and epilepsies, by external operation. London, F. Isted, 1724

Franklin, Benjamin (1706–1790) Maxims on the preservation of health and the prevention of diseases. Selected from the best authorities. With, The Way to Health from Dr. Franklin. From Lee & Co.'s Patent and Family Medicine Store, No. 33, Market-Street, Baltimore. Sold by William Y. Birch, Philadelphia (n.d., possibly 1813) and also, The Autobiography for references to George Cheyne, Thomas Tryon, Cotton Mather, John Fothergill, Cicero, others, and publication of Logan's translation of De Senectute, 1744

Galen, (ca. 130–200) De sanitate tuenda libri sex. Thoma Linacro Anglo interprete. Parisius, Impr. per G. Rubeum, 1517

Gompertz, Benjamin J (1779–1865) Diss. de dispositione corporis humani ad longaevitatem ex signis generalioribus sanitatis optimae. Lugduni. Bat. 1732

Haller, Victor Albrecht von (1708–1777) Elementa physiologiae corporis humani. Tom. VIII Pars secunda, Liber xxx. Vita humana et mors. Leyden, pp 48–124, 1766

Harcouet, de Longeville (ca. 1660–1720) Histoire des personnes qui ont vecu plusieurs siècles et qui ont rajeuni, avec le sécret du rajeunissement, tire D'Arnould de Villemeine et des regles pour conserver en santé et pour parvenir à un grand âge. Paris, Veuve Charpentier, 1714

Harvey, William (1578–1657) Anatomia Thomae Parri annum centesimum quinquagesimum secundum et novem menses agentis. Cum Guliellmi Harvaei aliorumque adstantium medicorum regiorum observationibus, in, Betto, J. De ortu et natura sanguinis. Londini, apud Guliellmum Grantham, 1669

Helmont, Joanne Baptista van (1577–1644) Ortus medicinae, id est, initia physicae inaudita. Progressus medicinae novus, in morborum ultionem, ad vitam longam. Edente authoris filio, Francisco Mercurio van Helmont, cum ejus praefatione ex Belgico translatâ. Amsterdami apud L. Elzevirium, 1648

Hill, John (1716?–1775) The old man's guide to health and longer life; with rules for diet, exercise, and physic; for preserving a good constitution, and preventing disorders in a bad one, 3rd ed. London, M. Cooper, 1750

Hippocrates (ca. 460–370 B.C.) De natura hominis: De victu; De tuenda valetudine; Medicinae lex; Iusjurandum; Demonstratio quod artes sunt; Invectiva in obtrectatores medicinae. Ed. and trans. by Andreas Brentius. Rome, E. Silber, 1480

Hoffmann, Friedrich (1660–1742) Diss. de valetudine senum tuenda; exp. Nitschius. Halae M., Tom. V, 1725

Hufeland, Christoph Wilhelm (1762–1836) Die Kunst das menschliche Leben zu verlängern. Wien und Prag, Franz Haas, 1797

Humphry, Sir George Murray (1820–1896) Old age and changes incidental to it. The annual oration delivered before the Medical Society of London, May 4th, 1885. *In,* Old Age, Cambridge, Macmillan & Bowes, 1885

Kiev: CTAPOCTb Proceedings of Congress on Aging, Kiev, December 17–19, 1938. USSR, Academy of Medical Sciences, Recklama, 1940

Lessius, Leonardus (1554–1623) Hygiasticon seu vera ratio valetudinis bonae et vitae una cum sensuum, indicii et memoriae conservandae. Auctore Leonardo Lessio, Societatis Iesu Theologo. Antverpiae, apud Viduam & filios Io. Moretti, 1613

Linné, Carl von (Linnaeus, Carolus) (1707–1778) Senium Salomoneum. Upsaliae, J. Pilgren, respondent, 1759, *and in,* Linné's Amoenitates academicae, V. 5, ed. 1, 1760; ed. 2, 1788, p 253–272

Lullius, Raymondus (Lull, Raymond) (c. 1235–1315) Tractatus brevis ... de conservatione vitae: item liber secretorum seu Quintae Essentiae qui doctrinam eius extractionis, et applicationis ad corpus humanum, et ad opera mirabilia totius artis medicae facienda, nec non ad metallorum transmutationem instituit; estque speculum et imago omnium librorum super his tractantium. Nunc primum in lucem edipus Strassburg; L. Zetzrer, 1616

Fig. 24

Christopher Wilhelm Hufeland (1762–1836): Hufeland of Weimar studied medicine at Jena and Göttingen. As honorary professor, he lectured at Jena on longevity and in 1797 published his two-volume work on macrobiotic, *The Art of Prolonging Life.* His historical, philosophic, medical, and hygienic views had wide reception in Germany where his disciplines gave it the name of the Hufelandist movement.

Mackenzie, James (?1680–1761) The history of health, and the art of preserving it; or, an account of all that has been recommended by physicians and philosophers towards the preservation of health from the most remote antiquity to this time. To which is subjoined a succinct review of the principal rules relating to this subject, together with the reasons on which these rules are founded. Edinburgh, W. Gordon, 1758

Maclachlan, Daniel (1807–1870) A practical treatise on the diseases and infirmities of advanced life. London, John Churchil & Sons, 1863

Maimonides (1135–1204)-Abou-Amram Moussa ibn Maimoun, Moses ben Maimon-De regimine sanitatis ad Soldanum Babiloniae. Florentiae, Monasterium, S. Jacobi di Ripoli, 1477

Maynwaringe, Everard (1625–?1699) Vita sana et longa. The preservation of health, and prolongation of life. Proposed and proved in the due observance of remarkable precautions. And daily practicable rules, relating to body and mind, compendiously abstracted from the institutions and law of nature. London J. D. 1669

Mead, Richard (1673–1754) Medica sacra; or, a commentary on the most remarkable disease, mentioned in the Holy Scriptures. Trans. from Latin by Thomas Stack. London, J. Brindley, 1755

Meibomio, Henrico (1638–1700) Epistola de longaevis, ad Serenissimum Celsissimumque Principem ac Dominum Dn. Augustum Ducem Brunsvicensem ac Lunaeburgensem octogesimum sextum annum agentem. Helmaestadi, 1664

Metchnikoff, Ilya Ilyich (Élie) (1845–1916) Études sur la nature humaine. Essai de philosophie optimiste. Paris, Masson, 1903. English translation, Nature of man; Studies in optimistic philosophy. P. C. Mitchell (ed.), New York, Putnam, 1905

Mettenheimer, Carl F. C. von (1824–1898) Nosologische und anatomische Beitraege zu der Lehre von den Greisenkrankheiten. Eine Sammlung von Krankengeschichten und Nekroskopien eigner Beobachtung. Leipzig, B. G. Teubner, 1863

Minot, Charles Sedgwick (1852–1914) On certain phenomena of growing old. Address before the Section on Biology, American Association for the Advancement of Science. August, 1890, 39:271–289 which predated his volume, The problem of age, growth, and death; a study of cytomorphosis, based on lectures at the Lowell Institute, March 1907. New York, G. P. Putnam's Sons, 1908

Morgagni, Giovanni Battista (1682–1771) De sedibus et causis morborum per anatomen indagatis libri quinque. Dissectiones, et animadversiones, nunc primum editas complectuntur; propemodum innumeras, medicis, chirugis, anatomicis profuturas. Multiplex praefixus est. Index rerum & nominum accuratissimus. Venetiis, Remondiniana, 1761

Mühlmann, Moisseis (1867–?) Über die Ursache des Alters. Grundzüge der physiologie des wachstums, mit besonderer berücksichtigung des Menschen. Wiesbaden, J. F. Bergmann, 1900

Nascher, Ignatz Leo (1863–1944) Geriatrics; the diseases of old age and their treatment, including physiological old age, home and institutional care, and medico-legal relations. With an introduction by A. Jacobi. Philadelphia, P. Blakiston's Sons & Co., 1914. (The term was used by him first in the article: Geriatrics, NY Med J 90:358, 1909)

Palaeoto, Gabrielle (1524–1597) De bono senectutis. Corona senum multa peritia: & gloria illorum timor Dei. Romae, Aloysii Zannetti, 1595

Paracelsus, A. P. Theophrastus Bombastus von Hohenheim (1493–1541) Libri quatuor De vita longa. Diligentia et opera Adami a Bodenstein recogniti nuncque primum in lucem editi, Basel, Apud Petrum Pernam, 1560

Ploucquet, Wilhelm Gottfried (1744–1814) Von menschlichen Alter und den davon hangenden Rechten. Tubingoe, 1779

Prus, Clovis René (1793–1850) Récherches sur les maladies de la vieillesse. Acad Roy d Med 8:1–27, 1840

Rembrandt, Harmenszoon van Rijn (1606–1669) For his many portraits of the old including, Old Woman with Prayerbook; Portrait of an Oriental; Scholar in a Room; Jacob teasing his grandchildren; his own parents, and the long series of self-portraits.

Reveillé-Parise, Joseph Henri (1782–1852) Traité de la vieillesse hygiènique, médical et philosophique, ou récherches sur l'état physiologique, les facultés morales, les maladies de l'âge avancé, et sur les moyens les plus sûrs, les mieux expérimentes, de soutenir et de prolonger l'activité vitale à cette époque du l'existence. Paris, J.-B. Baillière, 1853

Rush, Benjamin (1745–1813) An account of the state of the body and mind in old age with observations on its diseases, and their remedies. In, Medical Inquiries & Observations. Essay 10, On Old Age. Philadelphia, T. Dobson, pr. 1793, vol 2, 293–321

Sanctorius, Sanctorius (1561–1636) Ars de statica medicina. Aphorismorum sectionibus septem comprehensa, accessit statico mastix, sive ejusdem artis demolitio Hippolyti Obicii. medici et philosophi Ferrariensis, Lipsiae, Z. Schureri, 1614

Schlesinger, Hermann (1866–1934) Die Krankheiten des höheren Lebensalters. Wien, Holder, 1914. In, Nothnagel, C. W. (ed) Spez. Path. und Therapie, Suppl. V. 8–9, 1914–1915

Seidel, August (1863-?) Die Pathogenese, Komplikationen und Therapie der Greisenkrankheiten. Berlin & Neuwied: Heuser, 1889-translated, Diseases of old age, in, Wood's Medical and Surgical Monographs. 5:629–665, W. Wood & Co, New York, 1890

Seiler, Burcardus Guilelmus (1779–1843) Anatomiae corporis humani senilis specimen. Erlangae, J. J. Palm, 1799

Seneca, Lucius Annaeus (c. 4 or 5 B.C.–65 A.D.) De brevitate vitae, Eloge de la vieillesse, Epistle CVIII ad Luculium, c. 1492

Shakespeare, William (1564–1616) The complete works in which there are more than 125 old people including Adam, Polonius, Menenius, Gloucester, Lear, the Duke and Duchess of York, Juliet's nurse, Friar Lawrence, Falstaff and John of Gaunt and more than 1000 references to old age.

Shaw, George Bernard (1856–1950) Back to Methuselah. A Metabiological Pentateuch. New York, Brentano's, 1921

Sinclair, Sir. John, Bart. (1754–1835) The code of health and longevity; or, a concise view of the principles calculated for the preservation of health, and the attainment of long life. Edinburgh, A. Constable & Co.; London, T. Cadell and W. Davies, and J. Murray, 1807

Smith, Edwin Surgical Papyrus (c. 1500 B.C.) "The books for transforming an Old man into a Youth of Twenty," published in facsimile and hieroglyphic transliteration with translation and commentary in two volumes, by James Henry Breasted. Chicago, Ill., The University of Chicago Press, 1930, column xxi, line 9

Smith, John (?1630–1670) King Solomon's portraiture of old age. Wherein is contained a sacred anatomy both of soul and body, and a perfect account of the infirmities of age incident to them both, and all those mystical and aenigmatical symptomes expressed in the six former verses of the 12th chapter of Ecclesiastes are here paraphrased upon and made plain and easie to a mean capacity. London, J. Hayes for S. Thomson, 1666 (1st ed. 1665)

Stahl, Georg Ernst (1660–1734) Dissertatio inauguralis medica de senum affectibus. Halae. Magdeb. Johannes Conradus Michaelis, 1710

Stainer, Bernardinus (fl. 17c.) Gerocomicon, sive diaeteticum regimen, de conservanda senum sanitate, et vitae eorundem ad praefixum terminum productione. Nunc vero per Ioannem Neydecker, in gratiam omnium senum aut saltem ad venerandem senectutem aspirantium, in breviusculum tractatulum contractum. (per praxin sex rerum non naturalium) productione. Olim a Bernardino Stainer ... longiore atque confusiore modo conscriptum; nunc vero per Ioannem Neydecker genersum eius ... in braviusculum ... quendam tractatulum distincto ordine contractum atque concinnatum. Tractatulus certe tum utilissimus, tum lectu etiam iucundissimus. Wirceburgi, typis Eliae Michaelis Zinck, 1631

Stromer von Aurbach, Henricus (1482–1542) Schützrede und Verteidigung des ehrlichen und löblichen Alters. Welches von groben unverstendigen, unbillich verschmecht und gelestert wird. Wittenberg, G. Rhaw, 1537

Swift, Jonathan (1667–1745) Gulliver's Travels, Part III, A Voyage to Laputa, Balnibarbi, Blubbdubdrib, Luggnagg, and Japan. Chap. X. The Luggnaggians commended. A particular description of the Struldbrugs, with many conversations between the Author and some eminent persons upon that subject. New York, Doubleday, 1945

Temple, Sir William (1628–1699) Miscellanea. The third part. Containing I. An essay on popular discontents. II. An essay upon health and long life. III. A defence of the essay upon ancient and modern learning. With some other pieces. Published by Jonathan Swift. London, B. Tooke, 1701

Thoms, William John (1803–1885) Human longevity, its facts and its fictions, including an inquiry into some of the more remarkable instances, and suggestions for testing reputed cases. Illustrated by examples. London, J. Murray, 1873

Tossanus, Daniel (1541–1602) De senectute tractatus christianus et consolatorius. Heidelberg, Andreas Cambierus, 1599

Vacca-Berlinghieri, Francesco (1732–1812) Della nutrizione, accresimento, decrescimento, e morte senile del corpo umano. Si aggiunge Un metodo per preservare, e prolungare la vita ai vecchi, e due storie di alcuni Tumori dell'Abdome. Venezia, Giustino Pasquali, 1801 (first published in Pisa in 1762)

Venner, Tobias (1577–1660) Vita recta ad vitam longam: or, a plaine philosophicall demonstration of the nature, faculties, and effects of all such things as by way of nourishments make for the preservation of health, with divers necessary dieticall observations; as also of the true use and effect of sleepe, exercise, excretions and perturbations, with just applications to every age, constitution of body, and time of yeere. Whereunto is annexed a necessary and compendious Treatise of the famous Baths of Bathe, lately published by the same Author. London, publ. by the author, 1620

Voronoff, Serge (1866–1951) Étude sur la vieillesse et le rajeunissement par la greffe. Paris, G. Doin, 1926

Warthin, Alfred Scott (1866–1931) Old age, the major involution; the physiology and pathology of the aging process. New York, P. B. Hoeber, 1929

Weismann, August Friedrich Leopold (1834–1914) Über die Dauer des Lebens. Jena, G. Fischer, 1882

Willich, Anthony Florian (fl. 19c.) Lectures on diet and regimen; being a systematic inquiry into the most rational means of preserving health and prolonging life. London, T N Longman, 1799

Zerbi, Gabrielle (?1445–1505) Gerentocomia, scilicet de senium cura atque victu. Roma, ex officina, E. Silveri, 1489

ADDENDUM

In the literature on aging, old age, and the aged that is rich in talent, many works could have been undervalued, overlooked, or misjudged in the course of an arbitrary selection of a list of 100. In recognition of these possibilities, 20 titles have been added to compensate for the vagaries of judgment.

20 ADDITIONS

Boy-Teissier, Jules (1858–1908) Lécons sur les maladies des vieillards, faites à l'École de Médecine de Marseille. De la sénilité en général. Paris, O. Doin, 1895

Berger, Johann Gottfried de (1659–1736) Exercitationem inauguralem de morbis senum, ... p (roponit) Paulus Hofmann. Vitembergae, C. Schrodter, 1693

Burggraeve, Adolphe (1806–1902) La longévité humaine et moyens naturels d'y arriver. Paris, C. Chanteaud & Cie, 1877

Cuffe, Henry (1563–1601) The difference of the ages of man's life, together with the originall causes, progresse and end thereof. London, A. Hatfield, 1607

Day, George Edward (1815–1872) A practical treatise on the domestic management and most important diseases of advanced life. With an appendix containing a series of cases illustrative of a new and successful mode of treating lumbago, and other forms of chronic rheumatism, sciatica, and other neuralgic affections, and certain forms of paralysis. London, T. & W. Boone, 1849

Démange, Émile (1846–1904) Étude clinique et anatomo-pathologique de la vieillesse. Lécons faites à l'Hospice Saint-Julien. Paris, F. Alcan, 1886

Durante, Castore (1529–1590) Il tesoro della sanità. Nel quale si da il modo da conservar la sanità, & prolungár la vita, & si tratta della natura de' cibi, & de i rimedii de i nocumenti loro ... Roma, J. Tornieri & J. Biricchia, appresso F. Zannetti, 1586

Fitch, Samuel Sheldon (fl. 19c.) Six lectures on the functions of the lungs; and causes, prevention, & cure of pulmonary consumption, asthma, and diseases of the heart; on the laws of longevity; & on the mode of preserving male and female health to an hundred years. New York, H. Carlisle, 1847

Geist, Lorenz (1807–1867) Klinik der Greisenkrankheiten. Erlängen, F. Enke, 1860

Millot, Jacques André (1728–1811) La gérocomie, ou code physiologique et philosophique, pour conduire les individus des deux sexes à une longue vie, en les dérobant à la douleur et aux infirmités, par une Société de Médecins. Paris, F. Buisson, 1807

Mueller-Deham, Albert (1881–1971), S. Milton Rabson (1901) Internal Medicine in Old Age, 3rd ed. Baltimore, Williams & Wilkins, 1942

Ramazzini, Bernardino (1633–1714) L'art de conserver la santé des princes, et des persones du premier rang. Auquel on a ajouté, L'art de conserver la santé des religieuses, et Les avantages de la vie sobre, du seigneur Louis Cornaro noble Vénitien; avec des rémarques sur ce dernier, aussi curieuses, que nécèssaires. A Leide, Chés Jean Arn. Langerak, 1724

Rangoni, Tommaso Gianotti (ca. 1493–ca. 1577) Thomae Philologi Ravennatis [pseud]. De vita hominis ultra CXX annos protrahenda. Venetiis, Apud A. Arrivabenum, 1560

Rolleston, Sir Humphry Davy (1820–1896) Aspects of age, life and disease. London, Kegan Paul, French, Trubner, 1928

Sebizius, Melchior (1578–1674) Dissertatio de senectutis et senum statu ac conditione: instituta à Melchiore Sebizio. Argentorati, Welperianis, 1645

Stieglitz, Edward J. (1899–1956) Geriatric medicine. Diagnosis and management of disease in the aging and in the aged. Philadelphia, W. B. Saunders, 1943

Steudel, Johannes (1901–1973) Zur Geschichte der Lehre von den Greisenkrankeiten. Sudhoff's Archiv für Geschichte der Medizine und der Naturwissenschaften. Bd 35 H. i u.2, S. 1–27. Leipzig, J. A. Barth, 1942

Thewlis, Malford (1889–1956) Geriatrics; a treatise on senile conditions, diseases of advanced life, and care of the aged. St. Louis, C. V. Mosby, 1919

Trollope, Anthony (1815–1882) The Fixed Period. Edinburgh and London, Wm Blackwood & Sons, 1882

Van Swieten, Gerhard (1700–1772) Oratio de senum valetudine tuenda. Kraenzler, Vienna, 1778 (Rede über die erhaltung der Gesundheit der Greise)

3

The Historiology of Gerontology's Historiographers: A Classified Bibliography, 1900-1975

INTRODUCTION

The studies of gerontology's historians have become the guidelines for the scientific approach to senescence. Their accomplishments have inserted their names in the historical indexes and topical bibliographies of aging. The work and lives of these historians, each of whom is a "personal captive of chronology," as well as the subject headings and analyses about old age, are known to a smaller audience than should be the case.

In comprehensive catalogues of aging, there is a continuity in which seemingly unrelated and often obscure items of information get the classification that insures recognition. As directories of gerontology's publications become available, deficiencies in compilation, organization, and identification are eliminated. When sources of references are adequate, new and old remedies for longevity and a variety of programs of hygienic living are to be found. Roger Bacon, for example, in the 13th century hinted at methods of rejuvenation. A prescription for a way to restore an old man to youth was shown in the Papyrus Ebers, ca. 1550–1800 B.C. Proposals of ways to treat the old and to prolong life were not uncommon in the 15th and 16th centuries. Much of what then was known about old age was incorporated in the works of Magninus Mediolanensis which was of disputed origin ascribed variously to the elusive Magninus (fl. 1305), the great 12th century figure Arnaldus de Villanova and Mayno de Maynieri (d. 1368). The lives of supposed long survivors like Thomas Parr, buried in Westminister Abbey, and the Dane Drakenberg have been recorded. Their longevity is more likely to be apocryphal than factual. Texts on social (gerocomic) and personal (geriatric) health measures in the aging have become references for a growing number of students. The literature of aging has undergone a process of assemblage from remote times; its study never has lacked for protagonists. Evaluation of this material is being put into accessible form by students of the history of aging, that is, its historiographers.

Biologists not infrequently incorporated views on aging in their publications. In *The Treatise of Aristotle* that was translated and explained by Thomas Taylor in London in 1808 there is a chapter on the length of life with notes on old age. Gerontologists of centuries ago knew that the needs of the aging were part of the social deeds that had to be put on record. Many of those authors restated abstracts of the works of their predecessors.

Abstracts, translations, and commentaries on old age by the Judeo-Arabian physicians and other authors of the Renaissance rose in proportion to the growth of the population in which there was longer survival as social organization became more sustaining. The distribution of such information was stimulated by aspirations for health and longevity mocked gently by the famous painting of the Pool of Youth (Fons luventutis) by Cranach (1472–1553). Cornaro's brief treatise on temperance and sobriety went through many editions from 1558. All of Europe knew of Boerhaave's prescription for an old man to sleep between two virginal young women to regain health. Human milk was used as a rejuvenatory remedy. Efforts to transfuse the old with the blood of young animals and young people were attempted. The voyage of Ponce de Leon became legendary. Cohausen extolled the virtues of prolonged exposure to the abundance of healthy physiologic particles in the exhalations of virtuous young students.

In Sinclair's *Code of Longevity,* as has been cited, 1800 works on aging are listed, supplemented by abstracts, translated excerpts from ancient authors, national data, consilia, personal communications, some gossip, and pictures of many old people.

Although many able and eloquent clinicians by this time were on record on matters of aging, Charcot's authority and distinction initiated the modern era of gerontology in the 19th century. His summary brought an end to the classical period and introduced the modern era.

No longer is it possible for all minds to be current with all science or even major fragments of it. Special services need ready access to be effective, and bibliography is basic to the structure of a scientific field. It is, in fact, a good deal more; it is a part of that structure and testimony to the discipline whose development it marks. Every bibliography is an effort to advance studies a notch as a shorthand for others, and to create a perspective. The bibliography of aging that has been part of a cultural development marked by periods of inaction and neglect, even sterility, finally was propelled by the vigor that appeared early in the 20th century and took on increasing force by 1930.

A classified and critical bibliography of aging is a sine qua non of modern gerontology. Many students have been engaged in cataloguing the phenomena of old age. These expositions have been of help in the explanation of clinical reactions even when clinical identifications have lagged. Despite such deficiencies, data on senescence have contributed to the knowledge of the genesis of diseases and senescent reactions of the elderly, and also to methods of effective management. By the beginning of the 20th century there were more than 5000 major items in the bibliography of gerontology. Historians of this material have been a force in the development of the scientific field of the aging. Their contributions warrant a catalogue of their efforts.

A comprehensive selection of the works of the 20th century's historians of gerontology can be classified under 8 headings. Inadvertent omissions and questionable inclusions are inevitable. The effort was made to keep the errors to a minimum by reviewing the text of many articles about which there was a question.

1. Publications on the history of aging
2. Classical, modern and collateral gerontologists
3. Schools and institutions
4. Records of national data
5. Concepts of rejuvenation
6. Centenarianism and longevity
7. Classical citations
8. Miscellaneous publications

From the time of the Nei Ching of China, the Sushruta Samhita of India, and the Papyrus Ebers of Egypt, many scientists have contributed to the understanding of aging. Subjective approaches, empirical authority, random observations, and unquestioned generalities dominated the historical scene. It would be a mistake to conclude that the literature was only one of generalities. Sanctorius had ensconced himself on his scales and begun the assessment of body functions in terms of weight. Physiological measurements by Nicholas Cusanus (1401–1464), Quetelet (1796–1874) and Jonathan Hutchinson in 1846 offered prime examples of definitive measurements of age-altered effects.

In many instances, the personality of the authors often were more interesting and important than their thoughts. In the context of the times, awareness of the subject that kept it in the public and clinical mind justifies a catalogue of the historical writers. Each served a useful role. Remembrance of the past belongs in the realm of the full scheme of a growing discipline.

PUBLICATIONS ON THE HISTORY OF AGING

Recording the progress of the study of aging in all of its applications is not of recent date. During the 20th century, contributions to the study of senescence became more definitive. Publications disclosed a high degree of awareness of historical trends and creditable achievements.

Pioneers with a sense of the past and the future such as Nascher in 1914 and 1926 and Thewlis in 1918 wrote on the history of geriatrics. Both had included a review of the subject in their texts as Charcot had done more than a half century before them. The promise of the science of gerontology began to be fulfilled with the involvement of scientists like Cowdry in 1933. A brief history of geriatrics was published in 1939 followed by an authoritative series by Zeman from 1942.

Since that time, most of the data of the past on old age has been identified and much of the material has been subjected to an increasing number of critical evaluations. The rapid developments of the 20th century have become an integral part of the historical continuity of two thousand years of gerontic thought. Many items of this historical background are presented in a bibliography from the start of the 20th century. The publications are listed by author's names alphabetically. (In every instance in which a title has been found it has been the policy to check it for accuracy. When cross-checking confirmation failed in a few instances, the titles have been been identified with *nc*).

von Ackerknecht EH : Zur geschichte der geriatrie. Schweiz Med Wschr 91:20–21, 1961

Alvarez, WC: History of geriatrics goes back to 2500 bc. Geriatrics 19:701–704, 1964

Amako, F: A history of geriatric medicine. Acta Geront Japan 46:1–123, 1967

Amulree B: Twenty-five years of geriatrics. Br J Clin Pract 25:97–104, 1971

Beattie JW: The development of geriatrics. R Soc Health J 78:64–72, 1958

Bettencourt R: A velhice; pathogenia e therapeutica; a tradicao, a historia e a medicina. J Soc Med Lisb 69:3–35, 1905

Birren JE: A brief history of the psychology of aging. Gerontologist 1:69–77, 1961

Burstein, SR: Gerontology; modern science with a long history. Postgrad Med J 22:185–190, 1946

———: Care of the aged in England from mediaeval times to the end of the sixteenth century. Bull Hist Med 22:738–746, 1948

———: The historical background of gerontology. Geriatrics 10:189–193, 1955

———: Historical background of gerontology: "cure" of old age: codes of health. Geriatrics 10:328–332, 1955

———: The historical background of gerontology: Part III. The quest for rejuvenation. Geriatrics 10:536–540, 1955

Cath S: Psychoanalytic viewpoints on aging—an historical survey. In Kent DP, Kastenbaum R, Sherwood S (eds): Research, Planning, and Action for the Elderly. New York, Behavioral Publ, 1972, pp 279–314

Chebotarev DF: Ideas of S. P. Botkin and the development of modern gerontology. Sovetsk Med 31:142–148, 1968 (R)

Dawson-Butterworth K: Modern gerontology. Nurs Times 66:37–39, 1970

Dobrolowski L: History of geriatrics. Pol Tyg Lek 25:1328–1330, 1970

————: History of geriatrics. Geriatrics 26:68–9 passim, 72:76, 1971

Dry J: A travers la littérature gérontologique et gériatrique. Progr Med (Paris) 92:281–290, 1964

Duplenko L: History of the study of aging and old age. Vrach Delo 12:130–135, 1974

Editorial: The decades of geriatrics. Läkartidningen (Swed) 71:3061, 1974

Figallo-Espinal L: A contribution to the history of gerontology. Gerontol Clin (Basel) 14:257–266, 1972

————: Geriatria y gerontologia (Revision historica). Episteme 7:107–124, 1973

Finzi B: Contributo alla storia della geriatria a Venezia, Venezia, Huova Editoriale, 1964

Fraschini A: Silver anniversary with gerontology and endocrinology. Minera Med (Turin) 51:4352–4357, 1960

Freeman, JT: History of Geriatrics. Ann M Hist 10:324–335, 1938

————: The first fifty years of geriatrics (1909–1959). Geriatrics 15:216–217, 1960

————: Medical perspectives in aging (12th–19th century). Gerontologist 5:(Suppl 1): 1–24, 1965

————: Kiev to Kiev in Gerontology 1938–1972. Gerontologist 13:401–407, 1973

————, Webber I: Perspectives in Aging (Intro). Gerontologist 5: (Suppl 1), vii–ix, 1965

Gilbert C: When did a man in the Renaissance grow old? Stud Renaiss 14:183–192, 1967

Gold JG et al. Development of the care of the elderly; tracing the history of institutional facilities. Gerontologist 10:262–274, 1970

Goldstein A: Gerontology in ancient times. Harofe Haivri 34:176–181, 1961 (Hebr); 34:99–104, 199–207, 1962 (Hebr & Engl); also in, Koroth 2:596–597, 1962 (Hebr abst); Hebrew Med J 1:97–99, 1962

Grant RL: Concepts of aging; an historical review. Perspect Biol Med 6:443–479, 1963

Grmek MD: On ageing and old age. Basic problems and historical aspects of gerontology and geriatrics. Monogr Biol, (Junk, Den Haage) 5 (2):59–160, 1958

————: Les aspects historiques des problèmes fondamentaux de la gérontologie. Scalpel (Brux) 110:158–164, 1957

Gruman, G: An introduction to the literature on the history of gerontology. Bull Hist Med 30:78–83, 1957

————: The rise and fall of prolongevity hygiene (1558–1873). Bull Hist Med 35:221–229, 1961

Grynberg Z: History of the endeavor of medicine to prolong human life. Wiad Lek 21:279–283, 1968

Hinmen F: Dawn of gerontology. J Geront 1:411–417, 1946

Howell T: Origins of the British Geriatrics Society. Age Ageing 3:69–72, 1974

————: Geriatrics one hundred years ago. Med Hist 17:199–203, 1973

Kastenbaum R, Ross B: Historical perspectives on care. In, Howells JG (ed): Modern Perspectives in the Psychiatry of Old Age. New York, Brunner/Mazel, 1975

Kotsovsky D: Le problème de la vieillesse dans son développement historique. Riv di Biol 13:99–115, 1929

————: One hundred years of gerontology (a view backwards and forwards). Exc Med (Sect XX) Geriatrics and Gerontology 3:113–117, 1960

Krause L: Old age through the ages. Maryland Med J 6:680–682, 1957

Krogman WM: Changing man. J Am Geriatr Soc 6:242–260, 1958

Lawton AH: The historical developments in biological aspects of aging and the aged. Gerontologist 5 (Suppl 1): 25–32, 1965

Lüth P: Geschichte der Geriatrie. F Enke Stüttgart, W Germany, 1965

Mahdihassan S: The problem of old age in historical perspective. Medicus (Karachi) 31:129–133, 1965 (NC)

Marinesco G: Études historiques sur les mécanisme de la sénilité. Rev gen pures appliq (Paris) 15:1116–1129, 1904

McCay CM: Down through the ages. In, Cowdry EV (ed): Problems of Ageing, 2nd ed. Baltimore, Williams & Wilkins, 1942

Miles WR: Human personality and perpetuity. Gerontologist 5 (Suppl 1): 33–39, 1965

Munnichs JMA: A short history of psychogerontology. Hum Dev 9:230–245, 1966

Nascher, IL: Geriatrics (preface). Philadelphia, P Blakiston's Sons, 1914

————: A history of geriatrics. Med Rev: of Rev NY 32:281–284, 1926

Neuburger M: Zur geschichte der hygiene und prophylaktischen Medizin des Greisenalters. Wien klin Wschnschr 63:797–801, 1951

Pepper OHP: Geriatrics: past, present, and future (John H Musser Lecture). Am J Med Sci 223:589–599, 1952

Peret R: Geneza starosci (Genesis of geriatrics). (Pol) Polski tygod Lek 13:1665–1669, 1958

Postell WD: Some comments on early literature of geriatrics in America. New Orleans MJ 98:49–51, 1945

————: Some American contributors to the literature of geriatrics. Geriatrics 1:40–45, 1946

Randall O: Some historical developments of the social welfare aspects of aging. Gerontologist 5 (Suppl 1): 40–49, 1965

Reese H: Comments on the history of geriatrics. J Am Geriatr Soc 3:443–444, 1955

Robinson RA: The evolution of geriatric psychiatry. Med Hist 16:184–193, 1972

Rudy Z: Conceptions about old age in history. (Heb) Koroth 3:317–325, 1964 (NC)

Ruiz Moreno A: Notas para la historia de las enfermedades de la vejez. Hum Stud (Rome) 6:105–122, 1954

Schädewaldt H: Medizinhistorische Betractungen zur Geroprophylaxe. Veröff Dtsch Ges für Geront 4:1–9, 1970 (NC)

Simmons L: Aging in preindustrial societies. In, Tibbitts, C (ed): Handbook of Social Gerontology. Chicago, Univ Chicago Press pp 62–91, 1960

Stern K, Cassirer T: A gerontological treatise of the Renaissance "De Bono Senectute" by Gabriele Paleoti (1522–1597). Am J Psychiat 102:770–773, 1946

Steudel J: Zur Geschichte der Lehre von den Greisenkrankheiten. Arch F Gesch de Med 35:1–27, 1942

Steudel J: Gerokomie. Deutsches Med J. 3,4:89–91, 1956

Thewlis MW: The history of geriatrics. Med Rev of Rev NY 24:285–288, 1918

Veith I: Historical reflections on longevity. Perspect Biol Med 13:255–263, 1970

Valloi HV: Duration of life of prehistoric man. Comp Acad Sc 204:60–62, 1937

Verzar F: Concepts of basic gerontology of the past and future. Scand J Clin Lab Invest (Suppl 34) 141:86–88, 1974

Vischer AL: Einige gedanken über Alternsforschung Gerontologie und Geriatrie. Ztsch Altersforsch 9:219–222, 1955

Vojeova M: The fight for the prolongation of life. A historical study. Cesk Gynsk 30:417–421, 1965

Zanobio B: The locomotor apparatus in advanced age. Historical introduction (1) G. Geront. 18:995–1000, 1970

Zeman F: Life's later years: studies in medical history of old age. J Mt Sinai Hosp 11:45–52 May–June, 1944: 11:97 July–August, 1944; 11:224–231 November–December, 1944; 11:300–307 January–February, 1945; 11:334–339 March–April, 1945

———: Life's later years: studies in the medical history. J Mt Sinai Hosp 12:783–792 May–June, 1945; 12:833–846 July–Aug, 1945; 12:890–901 September–October, 1945; 12:939–953 November–December, 1945

———: Life's later years: studies in medical history of old age; nineteenth century. J Mt Sinai Hosp 13:241–256, January–February, 1947

———: Life's later years: studies in medical history of old age. J Mt Sinai Hosp 16:308–322, January–February, 1950

———: Life's later years: studies in medical history of old age. J Mt Sinai Hosp 17:53–68, May–June, 1950

———: Series of historical notes. Gerontologist 4:174–175, 1964; 4:220–221, 1964; 5:43–45, 1965; 6:173–174, 1966; 6:218–219, 1966; 7:75, 136–139, 1967

———: Some little-known classics of old-age medicine. JAMA 200:44–46, 1967

Zubin J: Foundations of gerontology: history, training and methodology. In, Eisdorfer C, Lawton MP (eds): The Psychology of Adult Development and Aging. Washington DC, American Psychological Association, 1973

CLASSICAL, MODERN, AND COLLATERAL GERONTOLOGISTS

Names of gerontologists can be divided into 3 groups and are listed alphabetically in the following subsections. In the first subsection, there are the names and references to the work of the classical students of aging who, for the most part, were active prior to the 19th century. Their studies on old age often were part of a larger corpus of their scientific observations but some took on a primary interest in the subject as their involvement expanded. In the second group there are the names, memorials, and records of more recent students of gerontology who had a special identification with the field as gerontologists. In the third section, there are collateral figures who made useful contributions to the knowledge of aging in science and art, and in general observations.

Classical

d 'Amida—Ruelle CE: Quelques mots sur Aétius d'Amida (a propos d'une publication récente). France Méd (Paris) 50:42–45, 1903
—Aetius d'Amida. (see Oribasius)
—Zerbos S: Aetius of Amida and his remaining works hitherto unpublished. (G) Iatrika Proos 12:8–14, 1907
Albertus Magnus (Albert von Böllstadt)—Stadler H: Irrtümer des Albertus Magnus bei benützung des Aristotles. Arch Gesch & Naturw (Leipz) 6:387–393, 1913
Aurelio Anselmus—Ceccarelli U: Un precursore della geriatria: Aurelio Anselmi Mantovano e la sua "Gerocomica." Atti Accad Stor Arte Sanit 27:155–172, 1961, S 11A
Aretaeus of Cappadocia—Cordell EF: Aretaeus the Cappadocian. Johns Hopkins Hosp Bull 20:371–377, 1909
—Howell TH: Aretaeus on disease in old age. J Am Geriatr Soc 19:909–912, 1971

—Robinson V: Aretaeus, the forgotten physician. Am J Clin Med 18:1055–1058, 1911

Aristotle—Osler W Sir: Aristotle. Can Med Assoc J 3:416, 1913

—Chandler AR: Aristotle on mental aging. J Gerontol 3:220–222, 1948

—Griffin JJ: Aristotle's observations on gerontology. Geriatrics 5:222–226, 1950

—Lüth P: Aristoteles und Galen über das Alter. Kapsel (Scherer) 1965 (NC)

Arnold da Villanova—Dusolier M: Los grandes medicos-filosofos catalanes: Arnaldo de Villanueva, Raimundo Lulio y Raimundo Sabunde. Gac méd de Granade 24:218–222, 1906

—Diepgen P: Studien zu Arnold von Villanova. Arch Gesch med Leipz 3:115–130; 188–196; 369–396, 1909–1910

—Diepgen P: Studien von Arnold von Villanova. Arch Gesch med Leipz 5:88–120, 1911

—Diepgen P: Studien zu Arnold von Villanova. Zweite Folge I. Arch Gesch Med (Leipz) 6:380–391, 1912–1913

Astruc—Osler Sir W: Jean Astruc and the higher criticism. Can Med Assoc J 2:151, 1912

—Simpson Sir A: Jean Astruc. Proc Roy Soc Med (London Sect Med Hist) 8:59–71, 1914–1915

—Zeman FD: Jean Astruc (1684–1766) on old age. J Hist Med 20:52–57, 1965

Avenzoar—(see Avicenna)

Avicenna—Chatard JA: Avicenna and Arabian medicine. Johns Hopkins Hosp Bull 19:157–160, 1908

—Cohen HM: Avicenna, Avenzoar. Maryland Med J 52:321–327, 1909

—Pitskhelauri GZ, Dzhorbenadze DA: Gerontology and geriatrics in the works of Abu Ali Ibn Sina (Avicenna). (On the 950th anniversary of the manuscript, "Canon of Medical Science.") (Russ) Sovetsk Zdravookh 29 (10):68–71, 1970

—Howell TH: Avicenna and the care of the aged. Gerontologist 12:424–426, 1972

Bacon, Francis—Steeves GW: Medical allusions in the writings of Francis Bacon. Proc Roy Soc Med (London Sect Med Hist) 6:76–96, 1912–1913

Bacon Roger—Elfferding H: Roger Bacons schriften über die kritischen Tage, mit einer Abhändlung über Bacons medizinis-

che Anschauungen eingeleitet und zum ersten Male nach der Handschrift in Erfurt herausgegeben. Erfurt, F Bartholomaeus, 1913
—Bacon Roger: Br Med J 1:1365–1367, 1914
—Roger Bacon and his cure for old age. Ann R Coll Surg Engl 18:286–287, 1956
Bichat X—Thayer WS: Bichat. Johns Hopkins Hosp Bull 14:197–201, 1903
—Blanchard R: Centenaire de la mort de Xavier Bichat. Paris, F-R de Rudeval, 1903
Boorde—Colwell HA: Andrew Boorde and his medical works. Middlesex Hosp J, London, 15:25–43, 1911–1912
Burggraeve—Leboucq H: Ad. Burggraeve, notice sur sa vie et ses traveaux. Belgique Med 13:291–294, 1906
Caelius Aurelianus—Merimer: Caelius Aurelianus: maladies aigues et maladies chroniques; le méthodisme. Janus Haarlem 11:129, 1906
Cardano—Cumston CG: Notes on the life and writings of Geronimo Cardano. Brit Med & Surg J 146:77–81, 1902
Celsus—Celsus redivivus. Lancet 2:904, 1904
—Barduzzi D: Sui codici e sulle edizione del libro "De re medica" di Aulo Cornelio Celso. Riv Storia Crit Sc Med Nat Faenza 1:11–13, 1910
—Lefas: Aulis Cornelius Celsus: Rep de Med Internat (Paris) 3 fasc 27:19–24, 1913
—Wellmann M: A. Cornelius Celsus: eine Quellenuntersuchung. Berlin, Weidmannische Büchhandl, 1913
—Garrison FH: Celsus. Med Pickwick 1:65, 1915
—Howell TH: Celsus on geriatrics. J Am Geriatr Soc 18:687–691, 1970
Charcot—Marinescu G: Charcot si opera lui. Spitalul (Bucuresci) 25:591–599, 1905
—Vallieri W: Charcot e la gerontologia. Pag Stor Med 7:25–30, 1963
—Freeman JT: A centenary essay: Charcot's book. Gerontologist 7:286–290, 1967
—Grinker, J: Biographical sketch of Jean-Marie Charcot. Chicago Med Rec 34:330–336, 1912
Cheyne—McCrae T: George Cheyne, an old London and Bath physician. Johns Hopkins Hosp Bull 15:84–94, 1904

—Howell TH: George Cheyne's Essay of Health and Long Life. Gerontologist 9:226–228, 1969

Cicero—Loomis F: De senectute (Marcus Tullius Cicero). West J Surg 52:175–181, 1944

—Loomis F: "De Senectute" (Marcus Tullius Cicero, 150 B.C.). Pacific Soc Obstet Gynecol (1943) 13:113–119, 1946

—Chandler AR: Cicero's ideal old man. J Gerontol 3:285–289, 1948

—Carp L: Cicero speaks on old age. Geriatrics 10:43–45, 1955

—Leon EF: Cicero on geriatrics. Gerontologist 3:128–130, 1963

—Leibbrand W: Ciceros Schrift 'Cato maior de senectute.' Z Geront 1 (1):5–10, 1968

—Jarcho S: Cicero's essay *On Old Age.* Bull NY Acad Med 47:1440–1445, 1971

Cohausen—Beauvois A: Un practicien allemand au XVIIIe siècle: Jean-Henri Cohausen (1665–1750). Docteur en médecine et en philosophie. Premier médecin des princes évêques de Münster (1700–1719). Doyen des practiciens diocese de Münster. Paris, A Maloine, 1900

—Beauvois A: Un critique médical au XVIIIe siècle: F. Ruysch et J. H. Cohausen. Sages-femmes et accoucheurs. Arch Gén Méd (Paris) 5:236–256, 1901 (ns)

Cornaro—Van Someren EH: Was Luigi Cornaro right? Br Med J 2:1082–1084, 1901

—Keser J: Cornaro et ses emulés modernes. Biblioth Univ (Lausanne) 111:287–298, 1906

—The method of Cornaro. Practitioner 76:593–599, 1906

—Van Someren EH: How Luigi Cornaro regained his health and lived 100 years, together with an introduction and an address on Luigi Cornaro's method. London, Ewert Seymour and Co, 1913

—Walker WB: Luigi Cornaro, a Renaissance writer on personal hygiene. Bull Hist Med 28:525–534, 1954

—Pitskhelauri GZ: Kornaro i ego "traktat o trezvoi zhini" Vop Pitane 28:86–88, 1969

—Calvo Melendro J: The elderly, age with a future: Cornaro, L. An Acad Nac Med (Madrid) 86:581–598, 1969

Cusanus—Schmitz C: Die Medizin des Nikolaus Cusanus. München med Wochschr 55:2210, 1908 da Vinci—Verdier H: Notes médicales sur Léonardo da Vinci. Aesculape (Paris) 2:13–18, 1912

—Belt E: Leonardo da Vinci's studies on the aging process. Geriatrics 7:205–210, 1952

—Belt E: Leonardo da Vinci on "The Hard Teeth of the Years." Gen Prac 19 (4), 1956; 19 (11), 1956

Day—Scott CJ: George Edwin Day and "diseases of advanced life." Practitioner. 214:832–836, 1975

de Bacquere—Elaut L: Benedikt de Bacquere en de zeventiendeeuwse gerontologie in zuid-Nederland. Sci Hist (Antwerpen) 3:179–189, 1961

de Gordon—Bell HI: The bibliography of Bernard de Gordon's 'De Conservatione Vitae Humanae.' Proc XVII Internat Cong Med (London) 1913. 23:325–337, 1914

de Moivre—Bett, WR: Abraham de Moivre (1667–1754). Med Press 232:551, 1954

de Pomis—Mecchia A, Florio L di: Cenni di geriatria in un' opera del medico umbro, Davide de Pomis (1525–1600). Pag Stor Med 10(2):58–62, 1966 (NC)

Du Laurens—Zeman FD: Du Laurens (1558–1609) J Gerontol 5:266, 1950

Eramus—Erasmus, longevité humaine. Intermed Chercheurs Cur (Paris) 41:12, 1900

Fallopius—Di Pietro P: Le lezioni "De partibus similaribus" di Gabriele Falloppia. In: Scritti in onore del Prof. A. Pazzini. Rome, E Cossidente, 1968

Fauchard—McManus C: Pierre Fauchard (1690–1759). Dental Cosmos 49:1233–1245, 1907

Floyer—Szczesniak B: John Floyer and Chinese medicine. Osiris 11:127–156, 1954

—Gibbs DD: Sir John Floyer, M.D. (1649–1734). Br Med J 1:242–245, 1969

Gunn JA: British masters of medicine, Sir John Floyer (1649–1734) Med Press & Circ (London) 189:297–299, 1934

Fothergill—Fox RH: John Fothergill. Practitioner 87:841–863, 1911

Galen—Harvey TW: Claudius Galen, 131 A.D. to 200 A.D. Med Rec NY 82:980–984, 1912

—Theoharides TC: Galen on marasmus With transl of text J Hist Med 26:369–390, 1971

—Galen. (see Aristotle)

Harvey—Cohen HM: Harvey. Maryland Med J 53:452–462, 1909

—Pearl R: Harvey's post-mortem examination of Thomas Parr. Hum Biol 3:138–142, 1931

   —Anatomy of Thomas Parr (transl reprint). St Barth Hosp Rep 72:17–22, 1939

   —(see Pitskhelauri)

   —Zeman FD: The old age of William Harvey. Mod Med 3:829–834, 1963

Hippocrates—Caton R: Hippocrates and the newly-discovered Health Temple of Cos. Brit Med J 1:571–577, 1906; also in, Lancet 1:695–697, 1906

Hufeland—Bois-Raymond C du: Ein auditorium-anschlag des alten Hufeland. Berl Klin Wschrschr 41:937, 1904

—Schenk P: Kant und Hufeland. Med Woch (Berlin)7:278–292, 1906

—Hänsemann D von: Hufeland und die Hufelandische Gesellschaft: Festrede. Berl Klin Wchnschr 47:243–248, 1910

—Sudhoff K: Christian Wilhelm Hufeland (1762–1836) und die "Hufelandische Gesellschaft" in Berlin, 1810–1910. München Med Wchnschr 57:250–253, 1910

—Pägel J: Zur altern Geschichte der Hufelandschen Gesellschaft. Eine Skizze. Janus 15:3–8, 1910

—Knorre H von: Justus Christian von Loder in Moskau. 12 ungedruckte Briefe Loders an Christian Wilhelm Hufeland aus den Jahren 1807–1831. Wiss Z Friedrich-Schiller-Univ Jena 7:419–447, 1957–1958

—Carrasco PT: Hufeland, Christoph Wilhelm (1762–1836). Hufeland, C. G. Macrobiotica o el arte de prolongar la vida del hombre. Introduccion y seleccion de textos por el Dr. Pedro Tellez Carrasco. Act lusa-esp Neurol 18:234–249, 1959

—Kloppe W: Christoph Wilhelm Hufeland's Macrobiotik als universelle Basistherapie. Zur erennergung an seinem 200 geburtstag [Christoph Wilhelm Hufeland's macrobiosis as a universal basis theory. In memory of his 200th birthday.] Deutsch Med J 13:515–516, 1962

—Pitskhelauri GZ: The macrobiotics of Christopher William Hufeland. (On the 175th anniversary of the publication of his work. "The art of prolonging human life.") Sovetsk Zdravookh 31 (6):77–80, 1972

—Rath G: Christoph Wilhelm Hufeland und seines "Makrobiotik": eine erinnerung an seinem 200 geburststag Ther Ber 34:144, 1960

Imhotep—The first physician I-Em-Hotep. JAMA (Chicago) 53:637, 1909

Laennec—Morgan JD: Laennec, the great internist. Wash M Ann 9:250–260, 1910–1911

Lessius—Boeynaems P: De eubiotiek van Lessius (1554–1663) of "Lessius; opuatting van de gezonheidszorg." Sint-Lucasblad NR 2:126–139, 1955

Linnaeus-Ebstein W: Carl von Linné als Arzt. Janus 8:115–122, 1903

—Church H: Linnaeus as a physician. Edinb Med J 10 n s:531–537, 1913

Lull—Raymond Lull. (see Arnold de Villanova)

Maimonides—Yellin D, Abrahams I: Maimonides. Philadelphia, Jewish Publ Soc, 1903

—Münz J: Moses ben Maimon (Maimonides) Sein Leben und seine Werke Frankfort/AM 1912

—Kahn M: Maimonides the physician. NY Med J 97:383–388, 1913

—Rosner F: Geriatrics in the medical aphorisms of Moses Maimonides. Postgrad Med 55:299 passim, 1974

—Rosner F: Moses Maimonides' responsum on longevity. Geriatrics 23:170–178, 1968

Mather—Cornwell HCD: Extracts from the diary of Cotton Mather. Postgrad NY 27:685–691, 1912

Morgagni—Piccinini P: Divagazioni nella storia della medicina: Gian P. Morgagni G. B. Ramazzini. Tribuna san Milano 1:36–40, 1907

—Zeman FD: G. B. Morgagni (1682–1771). J Gerontol 5:375, 1950

—Baptiste Morgagni. Scalpel (Bruxelles) 109:1159–1164, 1956

—Grmek MD: Morgagni und die Greisenkrankheiten. Sudhoffs Arch Gesch Med 4:117–128, 1960

—Spina, G: L'âge, la constitution et le tempérament en deux léçons inadites de Jean-Baptiste Morgagni. Scalpel (Brux)' 109:1159–1164, 1956

Oribasius—Cohen HM: Famous physicians: Oribasius, Aetius, Alexander of Tralles, Paulus AEginata. J Alumni Assoc Coll Phys and Surg 10:33–39, 1907

Paget—Putnam HC: A study of Sir James Paget in his writings. JAMA 40:97–98, 1903

—Marsh H: Sir James Paget; his character and his work. Middlesex Hosp J (London) 16:203–214, 1908–1909

Paleotti-Stern K, Cassirer T: Gerontological treatise of the Renaissance; "De Bono Senectutis" by Gabriele Paleotti (1522–1597). Am J Psychiatr 102;770–773, 1946

Paracelsus—Meunier L: Paracelse (1493–1541): la réforme en médecine au XVIe siècle. France Mèd (Paris) 52:163;180, 1905

—Cohen HM: Paracelsus. Maryland Med J 53:399–406, 1909

—Grasset H: L'histoire de la médecine et Paracelse. France Mèd (Paris) 53:341; 363, 1911

—Robinson V: Pathfinders in medicine, Paracelsus, iconoclast of medicine. Med Rev of Rev NY 18:40–51, 1912

—Newton RC: A short study of the career of Paracelsus. Med Rec NY 84:93–99, 1913

—Quecke K: Gerontologie und Geriatrie im Schrifttum des Paracelsus. Med Mspiegel 8:193–197, 1959

Parr—Pitskhelauri GZ: Postmortem examination of the body of Thomas Parr by W. Harvey. [Russ] Arkh Pat 31:77–80, 1969

Paulus Aeginata—Berendes J: Des Paulos von Aegina Abriss der gesammten Medicin in sieben Büchern, übersetz und mit Erklärungen versehen. Janus 15:9, 73, 143, 229, 463, 534, 622, 1910. Also, 13:417, 514, 655, 1908. Also, 14:33, 660, 1909

—Paulus Aeginata. (see Oribasius)

Plato—Griffin JJ: Plato's philosophy of old age. Geriatrics 4:242–255, 1949

Ranchin—Freeman JT: Francois Ranchin; contributor of an early chapter in geriatrics. J Hist Med 5:422–431, 1950

Rhazes—Cohen HM: Rhazes. Maryland Med J 52:282–288, 1909

—Ranking GSA: The life and works of Rhazes (Abū Bakr Muhammet Bin Zaharīya Ar-Rāzī). Proc XVII Internation Cong Med 1913 (London). 23:237–268, 1914

Rush-Cohen HM: Benjamin Rush and early American medicine. Maryland Med J 53:341–346, 1910

—Harvey TW: Benjamin Rush. Internat Clin Phila 4:232–243, 1912

—Woodbury F: Benjamin Rush, patriot, physician and psychiater: a centennial memorial note. Am J Insanity 70:941–944, 1913–1914

—Hader M, Schulman PM: Benjamin Rush: an early gerontological psychiatrist. Gerontologist 5:156–157, 1965

Sanctorius—Sanctorius. Nova et cetera (unsigned) Br Med J 2: 26–29, 1913

—Santorio, Santorio (1561–1636). Santorio Santorio–called Sanctorius. JAMA 184:968–969, 1963

Seiler—Rebmann E: Der menschliche Körper, sein Bau-und seine Tätigkeit; und Gesundheitslehre von H Seiler. Leipzig, GJ Göshen, 1906

Seneca—Kanngiesser F: Der tod des Sokrates und des Seneca. Oesterr Aerzte-Ztg (Wien) 9:56, 1912

Stephens—Gruman GJ: Doctors afield; CA Stephens (1844–1931) —popular author and prophet of gerontology. New Engl J Med 254:658–660, 1956

Stainer—Riedel C, Kramer H: On the gerocomicon by Bernardino Stainer. Gerontologia (Basel) 3:114–116, 1959

Van Swieten—Schoutene J: Gerhard van Swieten, a pioneer in the field of geriatrics. Gerontol Clin (Basel) 16:231–235, 1974

Van Swieten—Bergmeister: Gerhard van Swieten. Wien Klin Wchnschr 21:675–679, 1908

—Gerster AG: The life and times of Gerhardt van Swieten. Johns Hopkins Hosp Bull 20:161–168, 1909

—Rosaime: Van Swieten; jugé par Voltaire. Chron Med (Paris) 20:530, 1913

—Glaser H: Van Swieten's Rat und die Alten. Neuburger Festschr 11:190–192, 1948

Venner—Knott J: Dr. Tobias Venner; his Via Recta ad Vitam Longam. St Louis M Rev 1:245, 1904

von Haller—Hemmeter JC: Albrecht von Haller: scientific, literary and poetical activity. Bull Johns Hopkins Hosp 19:65–73, 1908

—Sudhoff K: Albrecht Haller. München Med Wchnschr 55:2142, 1908

Zerbi—Zeman FD: "Gerontocomica" of Gabriele Zerbi: fifteenth century manual of hygiene for aged. J Mt. Sinai Hosp 10:710–716, 1944

Modern Gerontologists

Allchin—Allchin Sir William Henry (1846–1912): Obituary. Br Med J 1:402–405, 1912; *Also in* Lancet 1:544, 1912

Balfour—Balfour George William (1822–1903): Obituary. Br Med J 2:439, 1903 *also in* Lancet 2:570, 1903

Baruch—Krusen FH: Simon Baruch, pioneer in the physical rehabilitation of the geriatric patient. Geriatrics 15:176–179, 1960

Bogomoletz—Frolkis VV: Development of AA Bogomoletz's ideas in modern biology of senescence. Fiziol Zh (Kiev) 17:352–356, 1971

—Halpern DA: Alexander A Bogomolets (contributor to problems of longevity). Am Rev Soviet Med 1:173–175, 1943

—Makarchenko AF, Kolchinskaia AZ: Development in the Ukraine of AA Bogomoletz's ideas on physiological aging and longevity in humans. Fiziol Zh (Kiev) 11:3–9, 1965

Botkin—Rozova KA: Vlad SP Botkin v razrabotku problemy starosti (Botkin's contribution to the problem of geriatrics) Klin med Moskva 35:68–74, 1957

—Chebotarev DF: Idei SP Botkina i razvitie sovremennoi gerontologii. Sovet Med 31:142–148, 1968

Bürger—Böhlau V: Das Lebenswerk Max Bürgers für die Gerontologie. Münch Med Wschr 112:2083–2086, 1970

—Bruch E: Max Bürger. Gerontologist 6:119–120, 1966

—Seide: Max Bürger, zum 80 Geburtstag. Deutsch Med Wschr 90:2126–2128, 1965

Burstein—Freeman JT: Sona Rosa Burstein: Gerontologist in motley. J Am Geriatr Soc 24:547–551, 1976

Cazalis—Faure J-L: Cazalis, Henri (1840–1909). Nécrologie Presse Méd (Paris) 17 (annex):553, 1909

Drysdale—Drysdale TM (1832–1904): Obituary. T Murray; Am Med 7:882, 1904

Durand-Fardel—Leudet: Éloge de Max Durand-Fardel. Ann d'Hydrol Climat Méd (Paris) 9:159–175, 1904

Fitch—Stoll HF: Dr. Samuel Sheldon Fitch, a New England consumption specialist of seventy-five years ago. Boston M & SJ 166:658–660, 1912

Greppi—De Nicola P: Enrico Greppi (1896–1969). (Ital) Minerva Med 60:10–14, 1969; Gior Geront 17:953–958, 1969

Henderson—Cole WH: In memoriam Edward Henderson (1896–1973). J Am Geriatr Soc 21:97–99, 1973

Hoffman—Strümpell A: Friedrich Albin Hoffmannzum 70 geburtstage. Deutsche Med Wchnschr 39:2258, 1913

Jalavisto—Holmberg PC: Eeva Jalavisto (1909–1966). Gerontologia 14:195, 1968

Kleemeier—Birren JE: Robert W. Kleemeier—gerontologist. Gerontologist 6:116–118, 1968

Korenchevsky—Cowdry EV: Korenchevsky, father of gerontology (1880–1959). Science 130:1391–1392, 1959
—Korenchevsky EV (1880–1959): Obituary, (with portrait). Gerontologie (Basel) 3:117–118, 1959

Lériche—Lériche René (1879–1955): Obituary. Ann R Coll Surg Engl 18:132–133, 1956

Metchnikoff—A propos des travaux de Metchnikoff sur le moyen de combatire l'atrophie sénile [La Presse génerale et les découvertes scientifiques.] *Med Obozr* (Moscow) 53:340–341, 1900
—Cancalon: Examen de la théorie de la vieillesse d'É. Metchnikoff. Chateaudun, 1904 (reprinted from *Rev Occident* 1904)
—Roux: Jubilé du professeur Metchnikoff. Ann L'Inst Pasteur (Paris) 29:357–363, 1915
—Besredka A: L'oeuvre de Metchnikoff sur la sénescence. Bull Inst Pasteur (Paris) 17:209–223, 1919
—Nagorny AV: I. I. Mechnikov in the campaign against premature senility and death. Vrach delo (No. 5–6) 25:229–236, 1945
—Meurs GJ van:Élie Metchnikoff (1845–1916): Voeding 25:351–356, 1964

Minot—Minot Charles S (1852–1914): Boston M & SJ 171:911, 1914
—Porter HT: Charles Sedgwick Minot. Boston M & SJ 172:467–470, 1915

Möbius—Bresler J: Möbius, Paul Julius (1853–1906). Nachruf Psychiatr-neurol Wchnschr Halle 8:395–397, 1906–1907
—Kollarits J: Die Philosophie von PJ Möbius. Heilkunde (Berlin u Wein) 103–106, 1907
—Strumpell A: Möbius Paul J (1854–1907): Nekrolog Deutsche Ztschr f Nervenh (Leipzig) 32:486–492, 1907

Moore—Birreman JV: Elon Howard Moore, pioneer in the sociology of aging and retirement. Geriatrics 16:626–628, 1961

Nascher-Thewlis MW: Nascher—father of geriatrics. Med Times 73:140–141, 1945

Parisot—Parisot P: Nécrologie. Rev Med L'Est 44:561, 1912

Pearl—Alvarez WC: Raymond Pearl, student of longevity (1879–1946). Geriatrics 14:56–58, 1959

Pflüger—Waller AD: Pflüger, Edward Friedrich Wilhelm, Obituary. Nature (London) 83:314, 1910
—Leo, H: Pflüger, Edward Friedrich Wilhelm (1829–1910). Nekrology München Med Wchnschr 57:1128–1130, 1910

Ray—Hader M: Isaac Ray, forensic medicine and geriatric psychiatry. Gerontologist 5:268–269, 1965

Rössle—Kotsovsky DA: Robert Rössle und die Altersforschung: zum gedächtnis des Prof. Dr. R. Rössle, gest. am 21. 1.1956. Münch Med Wschr 99:1510–1511, 1957
—Kotsovsky D: Robert Rössle als Altersforscher. Med Mschr 12:85–87, 1958

Robertson—Everitt AV: The work of Brailsford Robertson, a pioneer experimental gerontologist. Gerontologia (Basel) 4:60–75, 1960

Rübner—Lautz A: Max Rübner on aging. Geriatrics 16:44–51, 1961

Stephens—Gruman GJ: Doctors afield: CA. Stephens (1844–1931), popular author and prophet of gerontology. New Engl J Med 254:658–660, 1956
—Gruman GJ: C A Stephens: a pioneer of American gerontology. Geriatrics 14:332–336, 1959

Steudel—Steudel Johannes (1901–1973). In memorial. Med nei Secoli (3):425–426, 1973

Teissier—Teissier P: Le Professeur Potain. Rev univ Paris 52:1225–1228, 1901

Tarkhanov—Pitskhelauri GZ: The problem of longevity and the social hygiene views of I.R. Tarkhnishvili (Tarkhanova) Gig Sanit 30:57–59, 1965 (R)

Tuohy—Hirschboek FJ: Edward L Tuohy; a pioneer in geriatric medicine. Geriatrics 16:469–481, 1961

Verzar—Schlettwein-Gsell D: Fritz Verzár. Z Alternsforsch 22:185–187, 1969

Voronoff—Csillag I: Szergej Voronoff "a megfiatalito." Orv Hetil 107:1283–1285, 1966

Weismann—Conklin EG: August Weismann: Science (New York & Lancaster Pa) 41 n s: 917–923, 1915

—Gruenberg BC: August Weismann, the apostle of germ plasm, the life work of a great biologist reviewed. Sci Am 111:426–430, 1914

—August Weismann (1833–1914). Obituary. JAMA 63:2243, 1914

Zeman—Randall OA: Frederic D. Zeman, M.D. (1894–1970). Gerontologist 10:165, 1970

—Anon: In memoriam Frederic D. Zeman. Gerontologist 10:165, 1970

—Klingenstein P: FD Zeman (1894–1970) Mt Sinai J Med NY 37:654–657, 1970

Collateral Figures in Aging

Aristotle—Niebyl PH: Old age, fever. and the lamp metaphor (Aristotle), (Galen). J Hist Med 26:351–368, 1971 (and, The Helmontian thorn (J B van Helmont). Bull Hist Med 45:570–595, 1971)

Beard—Zeman FD: Beard's Legal Responsibility in Old Age. Its possible relationship to Sir William Osler's "Fixed Period" address. NY State J Med 54:1527–1529, 1954

Bright—Alvarez WC: A pioneer in geriatrics, R. Bright on diseases of the arteries and brain. Geriatrics 20:433–444, 1965

Cranach—Herrlinger R: Lukas Cranach: die alten am Jungbrunnen. Neue Z ärztl Fortbild 48 N F 2:368–9, 1959

Darwin—Schneck JM: Charles Darwin, William Osler, and "the fixed period." J Hist Med 18:175–176, 1963

da Vinci—Galeazzi M: Spunti di gerontologia Leonardo da Vinci. Ann Med Nav Trop (Rome) 58:378–386, 1953 (NC)

Davydovskii—Tiavokin VV: Concerning the work of Professor I V Davydovskii "Arterioschlerosis as a problem of age." Kardiologiia 7:143–144, 1967

de Léon—Olmedilla y Puig J: Pedro Ponce de Léon (al primero que enseño á hablar á los sordomundos) consideraciones generales acerca del mismo. Rev Med y Cirug Práct (Madrid) 94:129:172, 1912

de Renzi—Bazzi F, Manara R: Longevità nel clima della citta di Napoli in una breve nota di Salvatore de Renzi (1831). Considerazioni medico-sociali alla luce delle attuali conoscenze. Gior Geront 16:1395–1400, 1968

Goethe—Barach AL: The Goethean culture of experience—aging without abdication (Goethe, J W von). J Am Geriatr Soc 12:121–125, 1974

Holmes—Crothers SM: Oliver Wendell Holmes, the autocrat and his fellow-boarders, with selected poems. Boston, Houghton Mifflin, 1909

von Humboldt—Brednow W: Die problematik des alterns bei Wilhelm v. Humboldt. Zeit f Alternsf 14:89–93, 1960

Hunter—Pearl R: John Hunter on appetites and aging. Hum Biol 1:565–571, 1929

Jacobi—Jacobi A: Collectanea Jacobi. Robinson WJ (ed). New York, Critic and Guide, 1909

Joubert—Dulieu L: Le "cancellaria" de Laurent Joubert. Monspel Hippocr 1:16–22, 1958 (NC)

Montaigne—Cumston C G: The medical history of Montaigne. Albany M Ann 28:797–812, 1907

Osler—Ferguson J: Forty years and after: a reply to Dr. Osler. Can Pract & Rev 30:183–193, 1905

Parr—Darmstaedter E: Der alte Parr. Med Welt 7:722–723, 1933

Pelacey—Grmek MD, Théodorides J: À propos d'une thése sur la vieillesse soutenue à Montpellier par Augustin-Elzéar Pélacey, ami di Clot-Bey. Monspel Hippocr 30:21–24, 1965

Plato—Griffin JJ: Plato's philosophy of old age. Geriatrics 4:242–255, 1949

Ray—Hader M: Isaac Ray, forensic medicine and geriatric psychiatry. Gerontologist 5:268–269, 1965

Redman—McDaniel WB Jr: "Your aged friend and fellow servant, John Redman." Tr and Stud Coll Phys Phila 9:35–41, 1941

Rembrandt—Diekmeier L: Rembrandts alterswandlung im Spiegel seiner Selbstbildnisse; Beitrag zur Biomorphose der physiognomie (Rembrandt's aging as reflected in his self-portraits; a contribution to the biomorphosis of the physiognomy). Ztschr fur Alternsforsch 11:301–309, 1958

Shakespeare—Draper JW: Shakespeare's attitude towards old age. J Gerontol 1:118–125, 1946

—Vest WE: William Shakespeare, gerontologist. Geriatrics 9:80–82, 1954

SCHOOLS AND INSTITUTIONS

Some medical schools and institutions of health care have dedicated special efforts to the clinical considerations of older patients. Priority as a medical teaching center usually is given to Salerno but the Medical School of Montpellier, according to Garrison, was close to it in its founding in the 8th century A.D. After the Asklepieia of Greece, the Aesculapians made clinical observations that were included in the hippocratic corpus. La Salpêtrière and the Medical School at Nancy were involved in geriatrics at an early date in the 19th century. Modern teaching of gerontology in the 20th century began with Nascher's lectures at two medical schools as early as 1915, one year after the publication of his text. The development of a special journal on longevity in 1896 by C.A. Stephens and the organization of scientific societies on the subject in the 1940s are important parts of the field's development.

Alt KE: Neuer Beitrage zur geschichte der medicinischen Schule von Montpellier. Berlin, G Schade, 1902

Delmas P: La scolarité médicale de Montpellier au XVIᵉ siècle. Montpel Méd 37:169, 193, 217, 1913. Bull mem L'Acad Montpellier 1:57–75, 1913

Bettica-Giovannini R: Igiene dell'atto sessuale negli aforismi del "Regimen Sanitatis" della Scuola Salernitana. Rass-clin Ter 57:88–92, 1958

Bobbio A O: "Regimen Sanitatis Salernitanum" e seus preceitos higiénicos e estormatológicos. Rev Accâo med 4:23 1965 (nc)

Geller G: Die Geriatrie an der Salpêtrière von Pinel bis Charcot. Zürich, 1965. (Diss med Zürich)

Hader M, Seltzer HA: La Salpêtrière: an early home for elderly psychiatric patients. Gerontologist 7:133–135, 1967

Helme F: L'École de Salerne. Presse Méd (Paris) 18 (annex): 282–285, 1910

Herbeuval R, Larcan A: L'École gérontologique Nancètienne (1878–1913). Rev méd Nancy 81:549–567, 1956; Rev Franc gérontol 6:455–464, 1960

Marcuse J: Du Lehranstalt von Salerno und ihre Bedeutung für die Entwicklung des Medicinalwesens. Münch med Wchnschr 42:695–697, 1900
Moeller: L'École de Salerne du moyen âge et la Salerne d'aujourdhui. Chron méd Paris 13:97–103, 1906
The Medical School of Salerno. Br M J 2:946, 1904
Pic P: L'École de Salerne. Paris Méd 2(suppl): 17–27, 1913
Sudhoff K: Zum Regimen Sanitatis Salernitanum. Arch Gesch Med (Leipzig) 7:360–362, 1913–1914
———: Zum Regimen Salernitanum. Arch Gesch Med (Leipzig) 8:292–352, 1915

RECORDS OF NATIONAL DATA

There have been many compilations of data on aging in various countries. Easton in 1799 made a list of all of the long-living people that he could find, but it was done in an uncritical fashion. Sinclair's *Code* contained like citations. Thoms in 1873 had made an effort to distinguish between facts and fiction of claims of longevity. Records of Abkhasia and other geographical zones have been referred to for a century. Russell's study was an important effort to locate sources of material on longevity. Swift's story of the Struldbrugs was a critical and satiric precursor of the periodic "discoveries" of longevous groups in obscure parts of the world. From the list of 10 men after Adam whose lives were said to be an average of 800 years to the wide publicity about Colombia's Pereira, England's Parr, and Charlie Smith of the United States, the attraction of this subject never has waned.

Anatolia—Senjurik M S: Longevity of ancient inhabitants of Anatolia. Am J Phys Anthropol 5:55–66, 1947
Austria—Doberauer W: A special report: the evolution of geriatrics in Austria. Gerontologist 12:427–428, 1972

China—Chandler AR: Traditional Chinese attitude towards old age. J Gerontol 4:239–244, 1949
—Egerton FN III, Kutumbiah P: The Chinese and the Indian views on longevity and brevity of life: a comparative study. Indian J Hist Med 11:1–10, 1966
—Yuan IC: Influence of heredity on man, based on Chinese genealogy from 1365 to 1964. Hum Biol 4:41–66, 1932
—Weidenreich F: Longevity of fossil man in China and pathological lesions found in his skeleton. Chinese M J 55:34–44, 1939
Czechoslovakia—Tvaroh F: Development of Czechoslovak gerontology and geriatrics. Cas Lek Cesk 111:667–671, 1973
Denmark—Lund E: Gerontology and geriatrics in Denmark. Nord Med 70:885–886, 1963
Egypt—Zeman FD: Old age in ancient Egypt: contribution to the history of geriatrics. J Mt Sinai Hosp 8:1161–1165, 1942
—Buchheim L: Ein altagyptisches verjungungsrezept. Pharmalier Bayer 6:20–22, 1964
Finland—Javalisto E: Gerontology and Geriatrics in Finland. Nord Med 70:887–888, 1963
Germany—Probst C: Status and care of the old and sick brethren of the German Order of the Middle Ages. Hippokrates 37:736–741, 1961
Great Britain—Wigmore J: Medicine and its practitioners during the earlier years of the history of Bath. Bristol M & Chir J 31:193–212, 1913
—Adams G: Eld health, origins and destiny of British geriatrics. Age Ageing 4:65–68, 1965
Greece—Techoueyres E: La longévité dans la Gréce antique et quelques réflections médicales et biologiques. Sémaine Hop (Paris) 25:1034–1038, 1949
—Goldstein A: Gerontology in ancient times. Hebrew Med J 1:197–199, 1962
—Orth H: Diata geronton. Geriatrics in ancient Greece. Centaurus 8:19–47, 1963 (G)
—Richardson BE: Old age among the ancient Greeks. Johns Hopkins Univ Studies in Archaeology #16:1–376, 1933
India—Dikshit GS: The Sivattvaratnakara as the source for sciences in ancient and medieval India. Indian J Hist Sc 4:11–14, 1969

Italy—Necchi Della Silva A: A page from the history of gerontology in Milan in the second half of the 18th century. Aspects of admission to the old age homes (1). Acta Geront (Milano) 17:43–54, 1967

—Bazzi F, Manara R: Longevità nel clima della città di Napoli in una breve nota di Salvatore de Renzi (1831). Considerazioni medico-sociali alla luce delle attuali conoscenzi. G Geront 16:1395–1400, 1968

Norway—Gaustad V: Gerontology and Geriatrics in Norway Nord Med 70:888–891, 1963

Poland—Dobrowolski L: Development of geriatrics in the world and prospects of its development in Poland. Wiak lek 21:1265–1269, 1968

Rome—Editorial: Expectation of life in ancient Rome. Lancet 2:1784, 1913

Scotland—Ferguson T: A note on mortality in the islands of Barra and Tiree during the second half of the nineteenth century. Scot Med J 7:16–21, 1962

South America—Ilering von H: Das alter des menschens in Sud Amerika. Ztsch für Ethnol (Berlin) 46:249–266, 1914

Sweden—Eckerström S: Gerontology work and geriatrics in Sweden. Nord Med 70:892–893, 1963

U.S.S.R.—Alpatov V: Geriatrics in the Soviet Union. Geriatrics 20:348–350, 1965

—Tschebotarev DF (Chebotarev): Gerontologiens utveckling i Sovjetunionen (The development of Gerontology in the Soviet Union). Nord Med 73:453–455, 1965

Tschebotarev (Cheboterev): Gerontologie in aller Welt. Ztschv F. Alternsforschung 21:283–290, 1969

—Marchuk PD: Development of gerontology in the Ukrainian SSR. Fiziol ZH (Kiev) 13:698–704, 1967

—Editorial. Gerontology in Russia. Med J Australia 60:420, 1973

—Longevity in Russia. Sovet Vrach Zhur 4:205–216, 1941

U.S.—Postell WD: Some comments on the early literature of geriatrics in America. New Orleans M and SJ 98:49–51, 1945

—Postell WD: Some American contributions to the literature of geriatrics. Geriatrics 1:41–45, 1946

Venezuela—Figallo-Espinal L: Geriatrics in Venezuela. Geront Clin (Basel) 7:227–230, 1965

Western Society—Bower HM: Old age in Western Society. Med J
   Aust 2:285–292; 325–332, 1964

CONCEPTS OF REJUVENATION

The struggle to survive has been equated with quests to
reverse aging processes in which the masculine restoration of sexual vigor often is emphasized. Rejuvenatory
efforts have included endless measures of a physical, nutritional, substitutive, and arcane nature. Human milk,
qualities of mysterious waters, blood transfusions from
young to old, and many bizarre measures have vied with
sound admonitions to observe a temperate and hygienic
life as a way to maintain vitality. The control of infections
and the reduction in social strains have been reflected in
new attitudes and the assignment of a new sense of values
towards the elderly. The rate of the progression of senescent changes has been modified by increased accessibility
to good nutrition, secured opportunities for leisure, and
widespread effective public health measures.

Although the popular term refers to rejuvenation in
which a degree of reeroticization is implied, social goals
have been aimed at a longer span of well-being in which
there is more assurance of the healthy prolongation of life
for more individuals from birth. Rejuvenation takes on a
new synonym; it is the herald of longevity in physiological
balance and maintained health.

Borrowed youth. Organotherapy. The strange quest for rejuvena-
   tion. MD Newsmag 5 (9):204–208, 1961
Codellas PS: Rejuvenation and satyricons of yesterday. Ann Med
   Hist 6:510–520, 1934
Corneis GF: Rejuvenation-how Steinach makes people young.
   New York, T Seltzer, 1923
Csillag I: Sergei Voronov, the "rejuvenator." Orv Hetil 107: 1283–
   1285, 1966

Foundation of fantasy. Man's age-old quest for the fountain of youth. MD Newsmag 5 (9):200–202, 1961

Haire N: Rejuvenation, the work of Steinach, Voronoff and others. London, Allen and Unwin, 1924

Konkle WB: Revivification in legend. Dietet Hyg Gaz 28:295–298, 1912

Meyer B: Human milk as agent of rejuvenation in year 1500. Ztschr f Fleisch-u.-Milchhyg 38:266–267, 1928

Nascher IL: Longevity and rejuvenescence. NY Med J 98:61–65, 1913

Pezold von: Goethe's remarks on rejuvenation. Deutsche med Wchnschr 58:1099–1100, 1932

Quest for youth. Age old problem of human rejuvenation. MD Newsmag 2 (8): 86–88, 1958

Riddell WR: Virtue of breath of virgins in prolonging life. Can J Med Surg 79:20–26, 1936

Scardigli G: Considerations anciennes et nouvelles sur les soi-disant cures de rajeunissement. Gior Geront 12:63–69, 1964

CENTENARIANISM AND LONGEVITY

In a way, the gerontologist has become heir to the statistics of centenarianism. In homo sapiens with a species lifespan of approximately 120 years, the advent of a centenarian continues to be a sign of distinction as if social rather than personal values were responsible. Among students of aging, it is common to state that Emperor Huang —ti of the Han Dynasty in China lived 100 years. Galen (131–200 A.D.) was said to have had a long life. Cornaro's 100 years, the Salem Massachusetts centenarian physician, Dr. Edward Holyoke, and the French chemist, Chevreul, who was at work beyond the 100 year mark vie with press reports and census figures colored by dubious reports of longevity in parts of Abkhasia, Afghanistan, and Ecuador. National figures for centenarians continue to be published in chauvinistic fashion which is about as far as science has come in this field.

Centenarians*

A centenarian. Boston M & SJ 143:613, 1900

A lusty centenarian. (Editorial) Bost M & S J 143:147, 1900

Boquel A: Michel Chevreul (1754–1845). Arch méd D'Angers 4:51–57, 1900

A centenarian. Lancet 1:273, 1901

Death of a centenarian. (Editorial) Lancet 2:1278, 1901

Death of a centenarian. Med Rec NY 40:857, 1901

Hoffman FL: The art of living a hundred years; morality, temperance, and industry. Sanitarian 47:237–243, 1901

A centenarian. Boston M & SJ 147:602, 654, 1902

A centenarian (aged 107). Lancet 2:562, 782, 1902

Two centenarians, James Ross aged 111, Patrick Hearney, aged 106 years. Bost M & SJ 146:530, 1902

Mujer (Una) de 121 años. Rev espec méd La oto-rino-laringol espân (Madrid) 5:137,1902

De Senectute: Boston M & SJ 148:139, 141, 1903

A centenarian. Boston M & SJ 148:512, 1903

Death of a centenarian. Med Rec NY 40:857, 1903

French JM: Centenarians in Massachusetts. Medicine 9:24–27, 1903

Three centenarians. Boston M & SJ 148:76, 1903

A physician centenarian. Boston M & SJ 148:352, 1903

Centenarian. Boston M & SJ 149:441, 1903

A centenarian family. Br M J (London) 2:1444, 1903

Picard L: Les Médecins centenaires. Gâz Méd de Paris 3:117, 125, 133–135, 1903

Hundertjährige in der Schweiz. Schweiz Bl Gsndhtspflg (Zürich) 18:5, 1903

Weber FP: Medals of Centenarians. Boston, P R Marvin & Son, 1903

Gotthilf O: Wie lebten die Überhundertjährigen Leute? Ernähr u Gesundh Leipz 1:87–89, 1903

A centenarian. Boston M & SJ 150:548, 1904

Centenarians aet 104 and 102. Boston M & SJ 151:554, 579, 1904

Centenarians and more. Med Rec NY 65:384, 1904 (Sophia Gab, aged 129; N. Raby, 131 years, 11 months)

*This list is in chronological order.

Holyoke F: Our first president, Dr. Edward A. Holyoke. Essex South District Medical Society. Boston M & SJ 153:599, 1905

Tichenor GH Jr: How to live a hundred years. Med Brief (St Louis) 33:619–622, 1905

A centenarian aet 102. Boston M & SJ 155:356, 1906

A centenarian. Boston M & SJ 155:523, 1906

Centenarians. Boston M & SJ 155:725, 1906

Roth E: Standisehre der Aertze von 100 Jahren. Med Woche (Berlin) 7:256, 262, 1906

Valle 7 Aldabaldi: Autopsia de una centenaria. Rev de Med Cirug Pract (Madrid) 75:394, 1907

Hernandez Briz: Autopsia de una centenaria. Rev de Med Cirug Pract (Madrid) 75:66–70, 1907

Centenarians. Boston M & SJ 156:90, 216, 1907

De Senectute: Boston M & SJ 158:139–141, 1908

Welgamood N: William S. Clark, centenarian. Good Health 46:416, 1911

Bell C: Centenarians. Med–Leg J N Y 29:70–72, 1911–1912

Yves-Roy Mme Georges: La longevité humaine, les centenaires. AEsculape (Paris) 3:279–281, 1913

Gould GM: Two families of six living generations. Am Med NY 12n.s.:644–647, 1917

Centenarians in California. Bull Acad de Méd 81:835–840, 1919

The oldest man John Shell, aet 131. Good Health 55:199–204, 1920

Kotsovsky D: A propos de la longevité humaine (Deux cas de centenaires). Riv di Biol 12:217–224, 1930

Darmstaedter E: Der alte Parr. Med Welt 7:722–723, 1933

Garrigues A: Voulex-vous vivre cent ans et plus? Echo méd du Nord 9:141–142, 1938

Sarton G: Hoefer and Chevreul (with excursus on creative centenarians). Bull Hist Med 8:419–445, 1940

Bruning H: Old age of famous physicians. Wien med Wchnschr 93:112–113 1943

Longevity from ancient to modern times. Statist Bull Metrop Life Insur Co #10 28:1–3 1947

Pressat R: The centenarians. Goncours Med 81:4309–4312, 1959

Monroe RT: De senectute. New Engl J Med 272:1100–1104, 1965

Zeman FD: Centenarian Physician. Acad Bookman 20:3–7, 1967

Longevity

Angel JL: The length of life in ancient Greece. J Gerontol 2:18–24, 1947

Armaingaud: Montaigne's philosophy conduces to long life. Bull Acad de Méd 89:255–266, 1923

Beauvois A: La médecine chimique et la longévité humaine; une curieuse décade de moyens propres à prolonger la vie. Arch gèn de méd Paris 6:240, 351, 480, 1901

————: Essai sur la longevité humaine; un curieux moyen de prolonger la vie; la gérocomique. N. Iconog de la Salpêtriere 14:62–83, 1901

Bernard: Longévité des savants. Chron Med 8:455, 1901

Bernstein HJ: The prolongation of human life. Prov Med J 16:211–248, 1915

Bosc de Vèze E: Traité de la longévité ou l'art de devenir centenaire; manuel des convalescents, manuel des gens bien portants. Paris, H Daragon, 1908

Bourgoin L: La macrobiotique à travers les âges. Union méd du Can 71:839–849, 1942

Brunton TL: An address on longevity and the means of obtaining it. Lancet 2:1330–1335, 1906

Caulkins JS: Lessons in longevity. Phys Surg 28:245, 302–311, 351, 396, 1906

Cobb, WM: Human longevity in fancy and fact. J Natl Med Assoc 46:107–112, 1954

Crisp WH: An essay of health and long life, published A D 1725. JAMA 58:1843–1846, 1912

Cumston CG: Macrobiosis and the Goddess Hygeia. Internat Clin 1:97–103, 1925

David J: The oldest doctor in the world. Indian Lancet (Calcutta) 21:574, 1903

David, Jean 1801–1904. Br Med J 1:1521, 1904

Dimu K: Kann der mensch länger leben? Grundprinzipien der Makrobiotik. Med Wschr 7:433–436, 1955

Drinkwater H: The longevity of eminent medical men. Practitioner 93:844–852, 1914

Edgar JD: The Old, Old, Very Old Man; or the Age and Long Life of Thomas Parr. Milit Surg 62:499–503, 1928

Egerton FN III: The longevity of the patriarchs: a topic in the history of demography. J Hist Ideas 27:575–584, 1966 (NC)

Erasmus: Longévité humaine. Intermed d Chercheurs et Cur. 41:12, 1900

Finot J: La Philosophie de la longévité, 2nd ed. Paris, F. Alcan, 1900

Fisher I: Lengthening of human life in retrospect and prospect. Am J Public Health 17:1–14, 1927

Forslund JA: Ett langt lif, enlight historiens vittnesbörd och velenkapliga iakttagelser. (A long life, according to historical and scientific observations). Stockholm, 1901

Freeman JT: The longevity of gerontologists. J Am Geriatr Soc 23:200–206, 1975

Gale FM: "Whether it is possible to prolong man's life through the use of medicine?" [with trans of Joubert's "Erreurs Populaires"] Bordeaux, 1578, Book 1, Chap 2 J Hist Med 26:391–399, 1971

Garrigus A: Old recipe for syrup supposed to prolong life. Echo Med du Nord 9:141–142, 1938

Grant Sir J: How to live, to prolong life. Canada Lancet 35:517–525, 1901–1902

Greenley TB: The longevity of people of seventy years and over living in the valley below the city of Louisville, called the Ponds Settlement, within the last half-century. Am Pract & News 32:84–86, 1901

Griffin JJ: St. Augustine on longevity of antediluvians. J Gerontol 2:137–147, 1947

Grmek MD: Les idées de Déscartes sur le prolongement de la vie et le mécanisme du vieillissement. Rev Hist Sci (Paris) 21:285–302, 1968

Gruman G: Longevity, In, Dictionary of the History of Ideas. New York, Scribner's Sons, 3:89–93, 1973

Hansemann von D: Ueber macrobiotik Berlin Klin Wschnschr 47:189–192, 1910

Henley BJ: The Art of Longevity. Syracuse, NY, BJ Henley, 1911

Irwell L: Methods of prolonging life; a brief historical sketch. Medicine 8:827–833, 1902

Kaufmann R: Problem of longevity from Gorgis to Carrel. Med W 11:557–559, 1937

Klein CH von: A review of longevity. How to live. Alma 12 1:14–38, 1903–1904

Kotsovsky D: Can duration of life be extended? Basic principles of macrobiosis. Med Monatsschr 9:433–436, 1955

Lasalle A: L'art de Vivre Longtemps en Bonne Santé, avec Préface par de Nabias. Paris O Doin, 1906

Ledgard WE: A remarkable case of longevity, 102. Lancet 2:947, 1887

Legrand M-A H: La longévité à travers les âges. E Flammarian Paris 1911

A long-lived family. Am Med (Philadelphia) 8:951, 1904

Longevity. Scot Med J 13:317–319, 1968

Longevity from ancient to modern times. Statist Bull Metrop Life Insur Co #10 28:1–3, 1947

McDaniel WB II: Benjamin Franklin's vision of the extension of life to antediluvian standards (Abst). Trans Stud Coll Phys Phila. 24:85, 1956

McManus IC: Life expectation of Italian Renaissance artists. Lancet 1 (7901):26–27, 1967

Metchnikoff E: Causerie [sur la macrobiotique rationnelle] Ann de L'Inst Pasteur 29:364–366, 1915

Some complexities of Methuselahem. Mass. Dept Pub Health New Engl J Med 292:808, 1975

Nascher IL: A little journey to the home of the oldest man in the world; who and what he really is. Med Rev of Rev 26:291–303, 1920

Pitskhelauri GZ: Problema dolgoletiia i sotsial 'no-gigienicheskie vzgliady. IR Tarkhnishvili (Tarkhanova) (The problem of longevity, and the social-hygiene views of IR Tarkhnishvili (Tarkhanova). Gig Sanit 30:57–59, 1965

Quaker longevity. Med Rec NY 59:298, 1901

Riddell WR: Dr. Richard Mead's account of 2 oldest men. Canada Lancet and Pract 83:177–179, 1934; Med Rec 144:467, 1936

Rodriguez A: Un caso notable de longevidad de 124 anos. Siglo Med (Madrid) 53:341–343, 1906

Romberg, E: Gibt es Mittel das menschliche leben zu verlängern? Deutsche Rev (Stüttg u Leipz) 3:139–153, 1906

Rosenthal JT: Mediaeval longevity and the secular peerage. Popul Stud 27:287–293, 1973

Rosner F: Moses Maimonides' responsum on longevity. Geriatrics 23:170–180, 1968

————: Geriatrics in the medical aphorisms of Moses Maimonides. Postgrad Med 55:229 passim, 1974

Rules for maintaining healthy and long life by a Chinese physician of the seventeenth century (L'art de se procurer une vie saine et longue par un médecin chinois de la 36ᵉ année de l'empereur Khang-hi an 1687 de l'ère chrétienne.) Hôpital 20:622, 1932

Rundle H: The oldest living Scot (James Grieve) celebrated his 108th birthday on January 1st. St Barth Hosp J (London) 15:72, 1907–1908

Russell FE, Lucia EL: Comparison of mortality in New England colonial town with that of modern times. Am J Hyg 9:513–528, 1929

The secret of longevity. Br Med J 2:1475–1476, 1903

Skrzpczak A: (Longevity of the Polish physicians in the XIXth century, in the period between the wars and at the present time.) Arch Hist Med (Warsaw) 32:192–203, 1969

Smester: Longévité humaine. Intermed d Cherch et Cur (Paris) 41:317–318, 1900

Spivak AD: Longevity according to Hebrew lore and tradition. Med Life 34:191–197, 1927

Stephens TG: Thoughts on longevity. St Paul Med J 7:899–902, 1905

The oldest man living. Good Health, Battle Creek. 38:409, 1903

Weber H: On means for the prolongation of life. London, J Bale, Sons and Danielsson, 1904; Br Med J London 2:1445–1451, 1903

————: Ueber Mittel und Wege zur Verlängerung des Lebens. Deutsche med Wschnschr (Leipz u Berl) 30:671, 709, 743, 780, 956, 994, 1904

CLASSICAL CITATIONS

Talented individuals who reflected the nature of their times have recorded a number of observations about aging. In poetry, drama, painting, historical analyses, and in fiction, all of the underlying characteristics of aging mankind have been described in ways that cross time spans. In the work of Shakespeare, for example, the 125 old people were shown in ways that told not only of Elizabethan attitudes about old age but were as humanistic as the Greeks, and as perceptive as modern physiologists. Cranach's fountain of youth caricatured all of the weaknesses and inappropriate and unrealistic drives for rejuvenation by society.

Rembrandt's self-portraits that showed his aging and those of other old people, the perfect features of da Vinci's drawings of old men's heads, biblical stories, Browning's poem, and Shaw's play about longevity among many works have revealed aging in all of its dimensions. Talented minds saw what scientists were to measure when technical skills became equal to artistic insights.

Alvarez WC: Ageless advice on aging (Editorial) Geriatrics 29:136, 1974

Becker RM: Psalm 90, verse 10. S Afr Med J 40:867–869, 1966

Brandt S (1457–1521): The Ship of Fools. Gerontologist 5:176, 1950

Bruas F: Le "dies eger" et les "régimes de santé" dans les anciens ouvrages liturgiques. Chron Méd 17:673–678, 1910

Ciceron: Caton l'ancien (De la Vieillesse) (trans P Wuilleumier) Paris, Societé d'édition "Les Belles Lettres," 1961

Dragstedt CA: Methuselah et al. Perspect Biol Med 12:419–428, 1969

Draper JW: Shakespeare's attitude towards old age. J Gerontol 1:118–125, 1946

Fedeli M: Alcune osservazioni di biotipologia senile nella iconografia etrusca al museo nazionale di Villa Giulia. L'Economia Umana (anno VII) 5:26–33, 1956

Fink-Errera G: Les vieillards dans la bible. Vie Med 45:81–90, 1964

Gillies HC: Regimen sanitatis, rule of health. A Gaelic manuscript (by John MacBeath). Glasgow, R Maclehose & Co, 1911

Greenblatt RB: A sacred and a profane view of aging; Koheleth and Shakespeare compared. J Am Geriatr Soc 11:419–421, 1963

Griffin JJ: The bible and old age. J Gerontol 1:464–471, 1946 (with correction) 2:71, 1947

Hinmen F: Dawn of gerontology. J Gerontol 1:411–417, 1946

Krause LA M: Biblical portrait of old age. Bull Sch Med Univ Maryland 27:117–120, 1942

———: Old age in the bible and poetry. Ann Intern Med 36:152–156, 1952

Leibowitz JO: The old age description in Ecclesiastes and its medical interpretation by Johann Heinrich Michaelis. J Hist Med 18:283–284, 1963

———: A responsum of Maimonides concerning the termination of life. Koroth 5:3–7, 1969

McKenzie D: The Ebers medical papyrus. Med Press Circ 92ns:501–502, 1911

Massedaglia L: Veronesi, anoni lombardi, miniatoro del "Tacuinum Sanitatis." Atti Accad Str Arte Sanitat 20:14–26, 1954

Masson L: La fontaine de jouvence. AEsculape 27:244, 1937; 28:16, 1938

Mehta PM: Old age and its infirmities as described in Sanskrit classics. Ind J Hist Med 3:7–11, 1958

Mrkos J: Arabic physicians and medical details in the Thousand and One Nights in the 13–15 centuries. Casip lék cesk v Praze 46:485, 512, 539, 567, 593, 1907

Nascher IL: Some geriatric aphorisms. Am Med 9ns 723–726, 1914

———: Baneful psalm of Moses. M Times and Long Island M J 59:209–210, 1931

Nesbit L: Tragedy of senescence as portrayed in Schnitzler's "Casanovas Heimfahrt." M Life 41:306–312, 1934

Neuburger M: The Latin poet Maximianus on the miseries of old age. Bull Hist Med 21:113–119, 1947

Petzsche H: Chr W Hufeland's "Makrobiotik" im Spiegel von Goethe's "Faust," insbesondere der Szene "Hexenkuche." Dtsch Gesundh-Wes 17:651–660, 1962

Randolph J: Koheleth, canonical clinician. New Engl J Med 259:389–392, 1958

Régis: La phase de presénilité chez J-J Rousseau. Encéphale (Paris) 2:246–250, 1907

Ricciardelli RM: King Lear and the theory of disengagement. Gerontologist 13:148–152, 1973

Savitz HA: Geriatrics in biblical and talmudic literature. J Am Geriatr Soc 13:360–364, 1965

Schelenz C: Molesta senectus, proverbs and aphorisms. Münch Med Schr 110:746–748, 1968

Shaw GB: Back to Methuselah, A Metabiological Pentateuch, Brentano, NY 1921

Simon C: En marge de l'automne de la vie, ou Victor Pauchot et Ciceron. Bull med Par 46:5–12, 1932

Sims RE: Green old age of Falstaff. Bull Hist Med 13:144–157, 1943

Spector SI: Old age and the sages. Inst J Aging Hum Dev 4:199–209, 1973

Starcke J: Die Suçruta Samhita, en de geneeskunde der Hindoes. Nosokimos (Amst) 8:729, 745, 761, 1907–1908

Strong LC: Jacobean view of old age. Yale J Biol & Med 25:147–148, 1952

Sudhoff D: Ein kurzes deutsches "bonum regimum" zur gesunderhaltung aus dem 15 Jahrhundert. Proc VII Internat Cong Med (London) 23:237–268, 1913–1914

Suolahti S: The attitude of people in antiquity towards old age. Geron 19:10–18, 1969–1970

Viets HR: Osler and "The Fixed Period." Bull Hist Med 36:368–370, 1962

Vischer AI: Einige gedanken über Alternsforschung Gerontologie und Geriatrie. Ztsch Altersforsch 9:219–222, 1955

White W: Re–echoes of Sir William Osler's "The Fixed Period." Bull Hist Med 5:937–940, 1937

Williams HE: Adding years to your life. New York, Hearst International Libr Co, 1914

Yves-Roy (Mme Georges): La longevité humaine, les centenaires. AEsculape Par 3:279–281, 1913

Zeman FD: The Ship of Fools. Gerontologist 5:176, 1950—(see, Brandt, S)

Zeman FD: Old Folks Day—Unique Mormon tribute to the aging. Gerontologist 4:193–194, 1964

MISCELLANEOUS PUBLICATIONS

Among the many works on the history of gerontology from 1900 (and certainly many more prior to that time) there have been contributions to the subject that do not fit exactly into the previous categories. The following items link the subsections that were established and are a part of the full substance of the subject that can help to systematize the study of gerontology through its self-generating historical developments.

Adler F: The Spiritual Attitude towards Old Age. New York, 1906

Azzolini G: Il ricovero di mendicita, Vittorio Emanuele 11 di Bologna, le Oo Pp. Annesse e l'ospedale Marcello Malpighi della loro origine ad oggi. G Geront. 8:65–71, 1960

Bandalin Ya G: A struggle of science with old age. Mosk, ID Sitin, 1903

Bandaline J: The struggle of science with old age. Med Rec NY 64:81–87, 1903

Bansi HW: Einige Kapital aus dem gebiet der Alterskrankheiten. Deutsche Med J 7:37–43, 1956

Barron JJ: The geriatric patient and the physician. Wisc Med J 67:114–116, 1968

Bean WB: Aging and achievement. J Lab Clin Med 79:689–692, 1972

Bloom M: Gerontological evaluation in the 21st century: a fable. Gerontologist 13:318–321, 1973

Bramsen A: Die kunst alt zu werden. Gesundh u Wort u Bild (Berlin) 3:74, 1906

Brüning H: Old age of famous physicians. Wien Med Wchnschr 93:112–113, 1943

Burstein SR: Aspects of psychopathology of old age revealed in witchcraft cases of the sixteenth and seventeenth centuries. Br M Bull 6:63–72, 1949

Cargill JF: The value of old age. Pop Sc Monthly 67:313–318, 1905

Carlson ET, Woods EA: Uses of the past X Aging and mental illness. Repr Ment Hosp Oct. 10, 10:27, (7), 1959

Carmel R, Copelman L-S: Préliminaires a l'étude de la gériatrie en pathologie comparée. Rév Path Gen 63:507–514, 1963

Cathelin F: Oeuvres de grands hommes pendant l'extreme vieillesse. Progr Med (supp illus) 44:25–27, 1929

Chebotarev DF: Geriatrics—a new section in clinical medicine. Terap Arkh 38:8–13, 1966

Coffman GR: Old age in Chaucer's day. Mod Lang Notes. 52:25–26, 1937

Coutela VR: The Pavlovian basis of old age. In, Kent DP, Kastenbaum R, Sherwood S (eds): Research, Planning, and Action for the Elderly. New York, Behavioral Publ, 279–314, 1972

Csiky I: From the Home for the Aged to the up-to-date Home Hospital for Gheorgheni, Romania. Orv Szle 19:56–59, 1973 and in, Rev Med (Turgu-Mures) 19:57–60, 1973

Cunningham WP: Vincula praeteritorum. NY Med J 98:958–962, 1913

Dalmady J: A nyaralásról a makrobiotika szempontjabol. (Spending the summer from a macrobiotic standpoint) Budapesti orv ujság 3:579–583, 1905

Delaunay A: De senectute 1960. Vie Med 41:779–783, 1960

Dexter EG: Age and eminence. Pop Sc Month 66:538–543, 1904–1905

Doberauer W: Hinweise zur Entwicklung und Bedeutung der Geriatrie. Klin Med (Wien) 11:429–446, 1956

Dobrowolski L: Critical survey of geriatric therapy. Wiad Lek 22:1829–1831, 1969

Ewald: Die kunst alt zu werden. Bl.f. Volksgsndhtspfl (München u Berlin) R Oldenbourg, 6:81–87, 1905

Fletcher H: Fletcherism, What It Is: or, How I Became Young at Sixty. New York, FA Stokes and Co., 1913

Freeman JT: Deceptions and fallacies in geriatrics. J Am Geriatr Soc 8:519–526, 1960

———: John S.—widower. (JA Duncan) J Am Geriatr Soc 18:736–742, 1970

Garrigues A: Voulez-vous vivre cent ans et plus? Écho méd du Nord 9:141–142, 1938

Gotthilf O: Wie lebten die überhundertjährigen Leute? Ernähr u Gesundh (Leipzg) 1:87–89, 1903

Grant Sir J: How to live, to prolong life. Canada Lancet 35:517–525, 1901–1902

Hagemann E: Zur hygiene der alten Israeliten. Janus (Haarlem) 12:369, 449, 1907

Hagen B von: Eine ungewöhnliche Spätaltersleistung des Isokrates. Med Klin 55:2068–2069, 1960

Hofmeier, HK: Der alte mensch auf briefmarken. Cesra (Baden-Baden) 5 (7-8):36–38, 1958

Hogner R: Daily bread and daily life, is the art of living long and remaining young. Stockh 5:164, 288, 314, 315, 1915

Houghton HS: De senectute Am Med 8ns:17–20, 1913

Kastler A: Evolution de l'âge moyen des membres du l'Académie des Science. Sciences depuis la fondation de l'Académie. C R Acad Sc (Paris) 276:65–66, 1973

Kathelin F: Oeuvres de grands hommes pendant l'extrème vieillesse. Progrès Méd (suppl illus) 44:25–27, 1929

Kennedy RB: The toll of the Presidency: a shorter life. J Mississippi Med Assoc 9:21–23, 1968

Kotsovsky D: Rhythm of aging. Acta med Scandinav (Suppl 307) 152:167–169, 1955

———: Kann der Mensch langer leben Grundprinzipien der Makrobiotik. Med Monatsschr 9:433–436, 1955

Kramer M, Taube CA, Redick RW: Patterns of use of psychiatric facilities by the aged: past, present and future. In, Eisdorfer C, Lawton MP (eds): The Psychology of Adult Development and Aging. Washington D.C., American Psychological Association, 1973

Kupagin N: Staroset i Smert po Ucheniyu Yestestvispîtatelei (Old Age and Death According to Naturalists) Moskva, 1907

Lehman HC: The production of masterworks prior to age 30. Gerontologist 5:24–29, 1965

Lister J: Commonwealth and common health—medical care in old age—Byron's lameness. New Engl J Med 263:399–400, 1960

Llopis JM: Gerontologia y Salud Publica XVII Asamblea de Salud Publica. Caracas, 1970

Lueth P: Kurze geschichte der gerontologie und geriatrie. Neue Z arztl Fortbild 48 N F 2:509–514, 1959

Metchnikoff E: La Vieillesse. Paris, A Davy, 1904

———: La Vieillesse. Rev Scient Par 5.S., 2:65, 100, 1904

Morgan LG: On drinking the hemlock. Hastings Cent Rep 0 (3) 4–5, 1971

Nascher IL: Importance of geriatrics. (letter) JAMA 63:2248, 1914

———: The neglect of the aged. Med Rec NY 86:457–460, 1914

———: Geriatrics, the Diseases of Old Age and their Treatment, including Physiological Old Age, Home and Institutional Care and Medico-legal Relations (with an introduction by A Jacobi [with an historical review]) Philadelphia, P Blakiston's Son & Co, 1914

Neuburger M: Zur geschichte der hygiene und prophylaktischen Medizin des Greisenalters. Wien Klin Wschnschr 63:797–801, 1951

Newton, PA: William Brown's Hospital at Stamford. A note on its early history and the date of the buildings. Antiq U 46:283–286, 1966

Penfield W: Pseudo-senility: Osler's dictum reconsidered. Perspect Biol Med 4:437–444, 1961

Price ML: Ancient and modern theories of age. Maryland Med J 49:43–51, 1906

Probst C: Status and care of the old and sick brethren of the German Order in the Middle Ages. Hippokrates 37:736–740, 1966

Quackery in London in the eighteenth century. Br Med J 1:959, 1913

Rico-Avello C: Ideas biologicas de Fray Antonio de Guevara. La geriatria y gerontologia en los escritos des obispo de Mondonedo. Medicamenta (Madrid) 22:348–352, 1964

Rigold SS: Ford's Hospital, Coventry (old age hospital). Archaeol J 128:251–252, 1971

Romero H: Gerontologists and public health workers. Rev Med Chil 99:507–516, 1971

Rosner F: Geriatrics in the medical aphorisms of Moses Maimonides. Postgrad Med 55:229 passim, 1974

Rudd T: Old age: the completion of a life cycle. J Am Geriatr Soc 6:1–9, 1958

Savitz HA: Geriatric axioms, aphorisms, and proverbs. J Am Geriatr Soc 16:752–759, 1968

Schelenz C: Molesta senectus. Sprichworter und Aphorismen. [Molesta senectus. Proverbs and aphorisms] Münch med Wschr 110:746–748, 1968

Schramm G: Kuan-yin mit der "Vase des sussen Taues." Pharm Ztg 116:1432–1433, 1971

Sherman ED: Geriatric profile of Thomas Jefferson (1743–1826). J Am Geriatr Soc 25:112–117, 1977

Speiser AM: Another culture, another time. J Am Geriatr S 22:551–552, 1974

Spezzaferri F: Regolamento del Pio Ospedale dei Poveri Settuagenari nella Arciconfraternita di S. Giuseppe de Bologna (1662). Pag Storia Med 11(6):62–64, 1967

Steudel J: Zur geschichte der Lehre von den Greisenkrankheiten. Arch f Gesch d Med 35:1–27, 1942

————: Gerokomie. Deutsch Med J 7:89–91, 1956

Striker C: In defense of old age. Cincinn J Med 52:83–84, 1971

Strong LC: Jacobean view of old age. Yale J Biol and Med 25:147–148, 1952

Sudhoff K: Ein kurzes deutsches "bonum regimum" zur Gesunderhaltung aus dem 15 Jahrhundert. Proc XVII Internat Cong Med, 1913; Sect XXIII 359, 1914: Arch Gesch Med (Leipzig) 7:359–362, 1913–1914

Spector SI: Old age and the sages. Inst J Aging Hum Dev 4:199–209, 1973

Torresi L: Could Protti's intramuscular blood injection be considered a tentative antisenescence therapy? G Geront 17:353–359, 1969

Vitale M: Afrodisiaci e anafrodisiaci ne "Il Tesoro della Sanita" du Castor Durante, confronti con il Regimen Sanitatis. Hum Stud (Rome) 7:191–198, 1955

Valloi HV: Duration of life of prehistoric man. Comp rend Acad d Sc, 204:60–62, 1937

Wicks S Sir: De senectute. Lancet 2:1614–1619, 1905

Williams HS: Adding Years to Your Life. New York, Hearst's International 1914

Yuan IC: Influence of heredity on man, based on Chinese genealogy from 1365 to 1914. Hum Biol 4:41–66, 1932

4

Classified List of Journals on Aging, Old Age, and the Aged to 1975

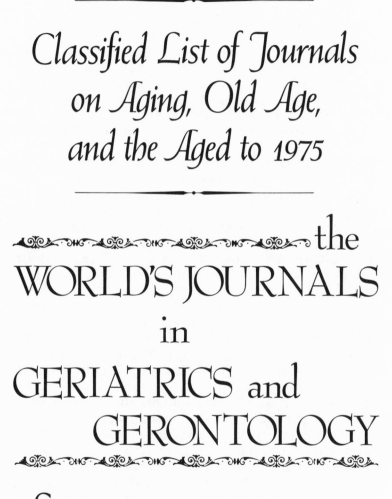

the

WORLD'S JOURNALS

in

GERIATRICS and GERONTOLOGY

*S*cientific journals serve special interests as guidelines for the dissemination of particular information and the establishment of standards. Continuity of publication is an expression of dedication by individuals and scientific societies in support of agreed-upon objectives. The scientific Gesellschaft lays down its prerequisites for articles that are acceptable and that are subject to editorial fiat. General reader and regular subscriber audiences including libraries are won or lost as circumstances alter typecases. In the 17th century, according to *M D*, "the medical journal was so-well developed that it became a permanent fixture, thanks to the printer's art, as a necessary instrument for the proper study and practice of the science and art of medicine and surgery and all the collateral branches."

Journals on aging have been mandated by clinical, biological, and social developments. The difficulty of a search into the past almost equals the problem of keeping up with the introduction of new publications. On several occasions it was thought by the author that an unequivocal starting point in this journal history had been attained only to be changed when additional titles were found. In the 1860s Mettenheimer and Geist considered collaboration "on a journal dealing with the physiology and pathology of the aged. With Geist's death in 1867 this first planned geriatric periodical was relegated to the future."[1]

Before the 19th century, numerous journals on health, hygiene, and longevity were available. In some of them, aging received index consideration as part of the general health directives. Wilhelm Christoph Hufeland (1762–1836) was a distinguished and authoritative German physician of wide influence. His *Journal der Praktischen Arznekunde und Wundarzney Kunst,* Jena, one of four that he edited, was published from 1795 to 1836. In 1797, this prolific student had published the two volumes of *Die Kunst das Menschliche Leben zu Verlängern.* With such interests, it would be thought that his journal would have many articles about old age. Despite general descriptions of diseases, forms of therapy, and other features of a comprehensive medical publication, there were no more than a few minor points about aging in the indexes of the first several volumes. With such limitations, it cannot be considered to be a precursor of journals on gerontology.

In 1919, Lacassagne referred to *Le Conservateur de la Santé*, a journal of hygiene and prophylaxis. It was published for five years from 1799 to 1804 in Lyon. The first volume, courtesy of the Bibliothéque Nationale of Paris, contained four pages. It appeared on the 10th, 20th, and 30th day of each month. Issues reviewed contained a number of articles on aging including an excellent one about a centenarian written by Dr. Brion and Dr. Bellay of Lyon. A photocopy of the first available issue was supplied by the Bibliothéque Nationale.

In volumes 4 and 5, there were the following:

"Essai sur la longévité et questions proposes sur ce sujet intéressant," n° 15 - T. IV (p. 113–118)

"La sobrieté est-elle une des causes d'une longue vie ?," n° 17 - T. IV (p. 129–134)

"De l'usage des frictions dans la vieillesse," n° 36 - T. IV (p. 281–285)

"De l'art de prolonger la vie," n° 1 - T. V (p. 1–5)

"De la gaité comme moyen conservateur de la santé," n° 19 - T. V (p. 145–151).

The 36th issue came out on the 5th month of the 12th year of the French Revolution's calendar. It contained a lengthy description of a centenarian, Jean Jacob, who died in 1770. Thévenin, a health officer of Lyon, wrote the story of the old man from personal knowledge. Such articles indicated a special interest in the hygiene and prophylaxis of aging and give this journal a high degree of priority among journals on aging.

A *Journal of Health* was published by the Association of Physicians in Philadelphia from 1829 to 1832. The issues contained a number of historical references, citations about health and longevity, instructions about diet and hygiene, reports of population growth, notations about exercise, and various directives for good health.

The Graham Journal of Health and Longevity (1837 to 1839) was the work of one Sylvester Graham (1794–1851) who was a clergyman and general agent for the Pennsylvania Temperance Society. He became interested in physiology and hygiene to obtain material for his temperance lectures. One-sided statements were made about a variety of subjects including aging. There were book reviews, health vignettes, and comments on subjects from urbane references to distinguished students of aging to the bad effects of wet feet. This magazine devoted the leading article in three issues to London's Thomas John Graham's: *An Account of Persons Remarkable for Their Health and Longevity* that was published in 1829. Two years earlier the same author had published *Sure Methods of Improving Health and Prolonging Life, or a Treatise on Living Long and Comfortably by Regulating the Diet and Regimen.* James Graham (1745–1794) had contributed to the field in his book *The Guardian Goddess of Health, Long Life and Happiness* published in Manchester in 1790. This Graham was a notorious quack who treated patients with medico-electrical apparatus and boasted of a Temple of Health and Temple of Hymen where the impotent and others of London were hoodwinked by claims for the beneficial qualities of a special rejuvenatory bed whose use commanded a substantial fee.

These journals are some of the many that represented their times. All of them referred to aging as one perspective of health but none can be considered to be a specific precursor of the type of journal that Mettenheimer and Geist had considered.

The 19th century saw a proliferation of scientific magazines as knowledge accumulated and particular branches of information were acquired by specialists. The first social journal in which aging was designated by title was *Old Folks' Record* published in Memphis, Tennessee in

October 1874, and terminated in 1875. Its aims were given in its salutatory, to "preserve the good of the past and present generation historically." Readers were asked to submit notes about old citizens, old neighbors, and traditions with special emphasis on items about agriculture

Fig. 25

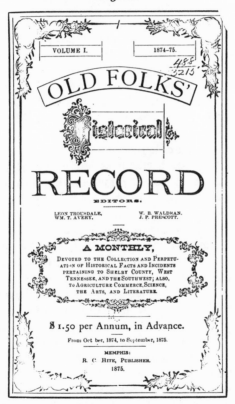

Old Folks' Record: Many organizations have published magazines that serve the interests of the elderly. This publication started in 1874–1875. It contained a number of items of interest to the aging as well as local features.

and manufacturing. The index listed articles on advice for old people to marry, notes about "father's growing old," a miscellany of homely 19th century news, and, of course, obituaries. There was nothing of scientific value in the magazine but the parochial articles heralded by its title made it a prime 19th century document about old age. No doubt there were earlier ones that failed to be located.

C.A. Stephens of Maine, who was graduated by Bowdoin College in 1869, was known initially for his many contributions to juvenile literature. He decided to become a physician and the editor of the *Youth's Companion,* Daniel F. Ford, financed his medical education at a homeopathic medical school in Boston. In 1883 the 39-year-old doctor-author moved to Maine. He built a large laboratory in 1890 where he began the study of cellular life in young and old dogs based on his hypothesis that cells could be made to live indefinitely. He was motivated to know "the course of disease, old age and death."

In 1895 he published the first issue of a journal, *Long Life,* from The Laboratory, Norway Lake, Maine. Its subtitle was: *The Occasional Review of an Investigation of the Intimate Causes of Old Age and Organic Death, With a Design to their Alleviation and Removal.* There was one more issue in the following year. Its table of contents (The Library of Congress has only Volume 2, 1896 of this publication) contained sophisticated references to heredity, multicellularity, capillaries in youth and old age, long- and short-lived cells, "the consentience of brain cells," questions about death, and a chapter on "Self, Cell self, and Multicellular Self." Dr. Stephens said that his journal was a "record and exponent of a special line of research ... It follows the progress and fortunes of laboratory work. . . . It will be printed whenever sufficient matters of interest have accumulated to make publication advisable." The idea of the journal had greater tenure than its lifespan. So far as has been determined *Long Life* was the first of its particular kind in the field of aging. Its projections and plans were far beyond its times.

Fig. 26

LONG LIFE

THE OCCASIONAL REVIEW

OF AN

INVESTIGATION OF THE INTIMATE CAUSES OF OLD
AGE AND ORGANIC DEATH, WITH A DESIGN
TO THEIR ALLEVIATION AND REMOVAL

CONDUCTED BY C. A. STEPHENS, M. A., M. D.

VOLUME II

THE LABORATORY
NORWAY LAKE, MAINE
1896

Long Life: C. A. Stephens was a major pioneer in gerontology. The titlepage of the second and final issue of his journal published in 1896 is reproduced. It was not possible to locate the first issue. The contents of the publication reflect Dr. Stephens's very modern views on a number of aspects of aging, some of which were studied in his laboratory in Maine, and others were subjects about which he was very well informed.

In September 1907, Hyland C. Kirk obtained a copyright for his journal *Longevity*. The editor's prospectus said that it was to be a "monthly journal devoted to life and physical immortality." Issues at 25¢ per copy were to contain material "relating to longevity and the improvement of life." The short-lived project of only two issues stated with assurance that "no one can say who buys a single copy of *Longevity* that he has not received full compensation for the investment." The table of contents for the first issue contained a number of historical allusions, an editorial on old-age pensions, reports of centenarians, demographic evaluations, "varying vitality in men," longevity of the settlers of Jamestown, and portraits of Captain John Smith and Pocahontas.

The Norwegian Public Health Association was founded in 1910 to focus on the nations's problems with tuberculosis, the period's leading cause of death. On the first of January of that year, its journal *Meddelelser (Information)* was issued. The incidence of tuberculosis and mortality from the disease abated as the result of improvements in public and social health. By 1949 the association's objective was reoriented to the new priorities of cardiovascular diseases and aging. The Norwegian Gerontology Society was founded in 1955 and issued *Norsk Selskp For Aldersforskning*. Both journals continue to be published.

In 1917 the *Medical Review of Reviews* of New York elected to have a section on geriatrics; Dr. I. L. Nascher was invited to be its editor. This appointment came eight years after he coined the word *geriatrics* and three years after the publication of his text under that name. The section was introduced as follows: "The diseases of the aged are worthy of the most careful study. . . . The *Medical Review of Reviews* appreciates the honor of being the first magazine in the world to contain a Department of Geriatrics." The claim undoubtedly was true for the title although clinical concepts and gerontologic ideas had

Fig. 27

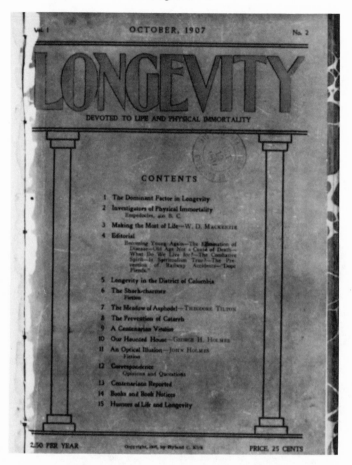

Longevity: The first issue of this private journal was published by Hyland C. Kirk in 1907. The volume 1, number 1 issue could not be located. This is a duplication of the front page of the second and last edition. (Because the journal was bound so firmly, it was not possible to obtain an unflawed reproduction). Courtesy of the National Library of Medicine.

Fig. 28

MEDDELELSER

fra

Den norske nationalforening mot tuberkulosen.

Redigert av
Nationalforeningens formand overlæge Klaus Hanssen
og sekretær dr. fru Elise Dethloff.

Nr. 1   September 1910   Aarg. I

Indhold: Nationalforeningens organisation. Konstituerende møte. Indlednings-
foredrag. Love. Valg. Diskussionsmøte. Plan for tuberkulosearbeidet.
Sanatorier og pleiehjem. Til og fra redaktionen.

Nationalforeningens organisation.

Paa det 13de almindelige norske' lægemøte i Bergen, august 1909 fattedes enstemmig følgende beslutning: Tuberkulosekomiteen bemyndiges til at ta de forberedende skridt til oprettelse av en norsk nationalforening til tuberkulosens bekjæmpelse.

Til sekretærhjælp bevilgedes 500 kroner.

Efter denne komites initiativ utsendtes i begyndelsen av juni 1910 følgende

Oprop.

Den norske nationalforening mot tuberkulosen.

Tuberkulosen er den sygdom, som for tiden herjer menneskeheten værst, og i alle kulturstater er arbeidet for at bekjæmpe den optat med kraft.

Ogsaa vort folk herjes av sygdommen; i tidens løp kræver den sine ofre i næsten hvert hjem; hvert aar tar den tusener av menneskeliv, oftest i den bedste og kraftigste alder.

Kampen mot tuberkulosen er ogsaa forlængst begyndt i vort land, og meget og godt arbeide er utført av den enkelte, av private foreninger og av det offentlige.

Men efterhaanden som forstaaelsen av denne kamps betydning for land og folk har samlet mænd og kvinder i voksende tal om arbeidet, har man i stigende grad følt savnet av en fælles organisation for det hele land, som kunde danne midtpunktet for alt det spredte arbeide og bringe enhet og kraft ind i dette, virke opmuntrende, hvor interessen ligger nede, veilede og gi raad til de enkelte foreninger og efter evne støtte deres bestræbelser.

I erkjendelsen av en saadan fællesforenings nødvendighet opfordrer vi medborgere til at tegne sig som medlemmer av den norske nationalforening mot tuberkulosen.

Medlemsbidrag mindst 2 kr. aarlig eller 50 kr. engang for alle.

Foreninger kan indtegne sine samtlige medlemmer mot et aarlig bidrag av 10 kr. for hvert hundred medlemmer eller dele derav.

Meddelelser: In 1910 the National Public Health Association of Sweden was founded primarily to focus on problems of tuberculosis. The publication *Meddelelser* (*Information*) was the Association's organ. In 1949, the objectives were re-oriented to include the care of the aged. The original title was maintained until 1963 when it was changed to *Helsenytt.*

received consideration in a number of special publications prior to that time. This magazine was incorporated with *Medical Life* of New York in 1937. The geriatrics section was a significant innovation for an established medical journal.

A magazine for the retired, *Voix du Rétraite,* was published May 5, 1921 in Paris. It was the result of a merger "of two publications that had been in existence from 1919 in which one already had this name." The August–September issue of 1974, #837, continued to have on its masthead, "Fondée en 1919." The publication, according to its

Fig. 29

⧗**GERIATRICS** UNDER THE DIRECTION OF ⧗
I.L. NASCHER

For the Study of Senile Conditions; The Causes of Ageing, Diseases of Advanced Life, Care of the Aged

I. L. NASCHER, the Father of Geriatrics in America, inaugurates herewith a department devoted to the important specialty which he has done so much to develop. Following his Salutatory he writes on the History of Geriatrics—history which he has helped to make. The diseases of the aged are worthy of the most careful study: an old man may be of more value to the community than a hundred infants. Let us not dismiss his ailments with the facile diagnosis: You are old. Pediatrics must be supplemented by Geriatrics. In this work Dr Nascher is the leader, and the MEDICAL REVIEW OF REVIEWS *appreciates the honor of being the first magazine in the world to contain a Department of Geriatrics.*

Ignatius Leo Nascher (1863–1944):   Few scientists at the beginning of a new field had the energy, intelligence, and foresight equivalent to this Austrian-born physician whose entire career in medicine was passed in New York. After he created the word *geriatrics* in 1909, he published a text on the subject in 1914, lectured in medical schools, worked in welfare institutions, wrote extensively, and helped in the creation of the American Geriatrics Society of which he was the honorary President in the last year of his life.

The Medical Review of Reviews (New York) invited Dr. I. L. Nascher to edit a Department of Geriatrics in its monthly issues. The announcement served the purpose of recognizing the priority of Dr. Nascher in the field and was an identification of editorial policy that was adding a new feature to an established medical journal.

editor, might well be accepted as the dean of special journals on the problems of pensioners. The 1921 copy was

Fig. 30

Le Voix du Rétraite: In 1919 this magazine was issued bimonthly for
two years when it was merged with another publication under this name
and has continued publication to date. It serves "for the material and
moral interest of retirees and future pensioners and for social reorga-
nization."

described as a publication that contained material of interest to present and future pensioners and to their social
organization. The pamphlet, originally a newsheet, contained articles on retirement particularly for state pensioners including military personnel. Its archives were
destroyed in World War II but a copy of the first issue was
located in the Bibliothéque Nationale in Paris.

In March 1923 the magazine *Pro Senectute* was published in Zurich by the Centralsecretariat of the Swiss
Foundation for the Aging. Its format was similar to other
house organs on aging containing material such as photo-
graphs of older people, letters, poems, book reviews, social

notes, quotations, and articles that would appeal to an older population of common background and interests.

In 1925 Yokufukai (Institution for the Elderly) in Japan was established as a juridical foundation to succor the old people who were left destitute by the great earthquake of 1923 in the Tokyo and Kanto areas. The new institution issued a publication *Yokufuen Chosa Kenkyu Kiyo.* The date of the first issue is in doubt (v.i.) but the second was in June 1931.

In 1954, with the 25th issue, the journal's name was changed to *Acta Gerontologica Japonica.* The dates of the journal's origin give it a form of priority in the history of publications on aging. Although not a clinical journal at the outset, continued publication showed an early aware-ness of the special needs and characteristics of elderly people, emphasized by the particular effects of a major catastrophe on them.

The journal has evolved into its current form. Its varia-tions have been traced through several sources in an effort to establish its place in the historical sequence of modern journals on geriatrics and gerontology.

The editor of *Yokufukai Geriatric Journal* wrote that: "The publication of our first issue was on December, 1928. However, it was not printed as *Acta Gerontologica Japonica* Volume 1." Dr. M. Murakami of the Tokyo Met-ropolitan Geriatric Hospital added (1978) that the "First issue of *Yokufuen Chosa Kenkyo Kiyo (Acta Geron-tologica Japonica)* was published by Dr. F. Amako, who died 6 years ago." The Reference Section, Serial Division of The Library of Congress reported: "According to the 1967 *Directory of Japanese Scientific Periodicals,* the pub-lication *Acta Gerontologica Japonica* began in 1930 with issue number 1. No title variation was noted in this refer-ence source. The Library of Congress' earliest issue is number 32, December 1960 and carries the title cited above." The Public Services Department of the New York Academy of Medicine said: "*Acta Gerontologica Japonica* was first published in 1930."

Fig. 31

PRO
SENECTUTE

Nr. 1

März 1923

Zürich

Pro Senectute: In 1910 the Swiss Foundation for the Aging began the publication of this little magazine which contains articles of particular interest to an older audience.

In the first book of Samuel, chap. 7:12, a site in the Holy Land was named Ebenezer after "the stone of help" that

Fig. 32

Ebenezer: The Ebenezer Foundation publishes this quarterly magazine which began in 1934. The Ebenezer Society has been serving the needs of the elderly from 1917 to the end "that the dignity and personal worth that each person be maintained in the caring program."

marked a place where divine intervention in battle had been helpful. In 1917 the Ebenezer Society was founded in Minnesota to help poor Norwegian elderly immigrants. The Ebenezer Gamlehjem or Old People's Home was established to house 10 people. In 1934 the magazine *Ebenezer* was created and is published as a house organ.

In 1923, the Bessarabian student of aging, Dimitri A. Kotsovsky, published *The Origin of Senility.* He was 27 years of age, a graduate of the medical faculty of the University of Odessa. In the same year he studied under the distinguished gerontologists Marinesco at the University of Bucharest, Besredka at the Pasteur Institute of Paris and then with Raymond Pearl of Baltimore and A. J. Carlson of Chicago. In 1935 Kotsovsky was granted a doctorate of medicine of the University of Vienna. In the same year he founded and funded the first International Institute for the Study of Old Age and published a magazine *Problems of Ageing* issued in five languages. Many world-famous scientists became honorary corresponding members of the Institute which had been recognized by the Rumanian government. More than 100 scientific institutions were in constant touch with the new journal and exchanged publications with it. The Institute closed in 1940 and the magazine was terminated.

The year 1938 was important in the development of gerontology. There was a National Congress on Aging in Kiev where Bogomolets and Basilevich were the keynoters. The first volume of the *Zeitschrift für Alternsforschung* was distributed. It ceased publication in 1944 and was resumed in 1951. The July 1938 volume was introduced as follows:

> The manifestations of aging always have engaged the interest of investigators in various fields of natural science and medicine. . . . until now there has been no comprehensive research into the causes and nature of aging. The publication of pertinent works in periodicals pushed far afield and often inaccessible doubtless has been injurious to the development of research in aging. The creation of a *new* periodical for a special field must be considered very scientifically. Before all else, what led to the foundation of this periodical was the conviction that the publication of a carefully edited periodical . . . would stimulate a broad and systematic investigation into the manifestations of aging.

The American Geriatrics Society was founded in 1942 with Dr. Malford W. Thewlis as a founder and permanent secretary. It issued its journal *Geriatrics* in 1946. When the title was preempted by the publisher, the official journal of the society continued as *The Journal of the American Geriatrics Society* in 1953.

The Journal of Gerontology, official organ of the Gerontological Society (1945) began in 1946. In 1954 the Society published a newsletter which was expanded in 1961 into a magazine form *The Gerontologist.*

The pattern of gerontology's major organizational characteristics was established by the time of the United States White House Conference on Aging in 1961. Many national needs were identified with special emphasis on organized training at all educational levels and the establishment of professional curricula. Several schools accepted fellows for study in gerontology.

The Older Americans Act signed into law July 14, 1965 and the activation of Medicare in 1965 helped to thwart the threat of almshouses or their equivalents and to underwrite forms of acute and long-term medical care. New phases of gerontologic development found outlet in journals that proliferated in quantity and sophistication. (At least three such were announced in the United States during 1975.) By 1975 specialization within the field of aging had begun in earnest. The field that had difficulty in acquiring topical identification in science had begun to develop its own special subtopics, adherents, and media outlets. The subject had become very fluid so that historical assessments were having difficulty maintaining pace with the new additions.

COMMENT

Lists of journals on aging and their classification are readily susceptible to errors and questionable decisions. Editors, policies, and titles of journals change, sometimes to come to the surface again in mergers or other forms that are not documented clearly. The date of a first issue may be difficult to resolve. Accessibility to documentation can be a troublesome factor across national boundaries. Sources may be at variance. Despite these and other limitations such as the overlapping of organization and community services that have added to the problem, a fairly satisfactory listing has been accomplished.

Postal communications by the author were used repeatedly to obtain confirmations, particularly from countries in which the dates of initiation, and sometimes of termination of journals and magazines, were not recorded unequivocally. Some of these inquiries failed but a majority were effective.

There are 4 classifications, namely, publications of scientific organizations and societies, social and government agencies, those of publishers independent of or affiliated with organizations, and those of organizations with the special interests of their older age community. So far as has been determined, this is the first time that journals on aging, old age, and the aged have been put into such categories.

The year of initial publication (and termination when known), name of the organization, agency or publisher, and city of origin when available, are recorded.

This classified list ranged from journals of preliminary or limited involvement in aging to those of major type that began up to 1975. The citations are significant for the long period of time in which specific journals have been thought of, and then became available, and also for their content expressive of the dedication to this subject long before its present established status.

Scientific Organizations

Acta Gerontologica, 1950–1974. Istituto Medicamenta S.A. Milan, Italy
Acta Gerontologica Belgica, 1963–1965. (see below)
Acta Gerontologica et Geriatrica Belgica, 1965? (formerly, *Acta Gerontologica Belgica*); Belgian Association of Geriatrics, St. Ideswald-on-the-sea, Belgium

Acta Gerontologica Japonica, 1928–1930. Japan Gerontological Society, (see, *Yokufuen Chosa Kenkyu Kiyo,* also *Yokufukai Geriatric Journal*), Tokyo, Japan [see text]
Actuelle Gerontologie, 1970 (continued as, *Aktuelle Gerontologie,* 1971). Deutsche Gesellschaft fuer Gerontologie and, Osterreichische Gesellschaft fuer Geriatrie, Stüttgart, West Germany
Age and Ageing, 1972. Journal of the British Geriatric Society and the British Society for Research in Ageing, London, England
Altersprobleme, 1937. Zeitschrift für Internationale Altersforschung und Altersbekampfung, Institutul Pentru Studiul si Combaterea Batranetii, Chisinau, Bessarabia, Rumania
British Journal of Geriatric Practice, 1962–1973. Proceedings of the S. London Geriatric Society, changed to, *British Journal of Geriatrics and Psychogeriatrics,* q.v.
British Journal of Geriatrics, 1962–1963. (see *British Journal of Geriatrics and Psychogeriatrics*)
British Journal of Geriatrics and Psychogeriatrics, 1973. Stuart Phillips Publications, Surrey, England
Geriatric Medicine, 1971. (see *Korei Agaku; Ronen Igaku*) Yen Life Science Company, Tokyo, Japan
Geriatrics, 1946. (Originally the official publication of the American Geriatrics Society and continued as a Lancet Publication from 1953; (see *Journal of the American Geriatrics Society,* 1946)
Geron, 1949. Societas Gerontologica Fennica, Helsinki, Finland
Gerontological Society Newsletter, 1954–1960 (succeeded by *The Gerontologist,* 1961) Gerontological Society, United States, Washington, D.C.
Gerontologiia i Geriatriia (annual) Akademiia Meditsinskikh Nauk SSSR. Institut Gerontologii, Kiev (Gerontology and Geriatrics, Kiev), USSR
The Gerontologist, 1961 (Successor to the *Gerontological Society Newsletter*) Gerontological Society, United States, Washington, D.C.
Giornale di Gerontologia, 1953. Societa Italiana di Gerontologia e Geriatria, Florence, Italy
Giornale di Gerontologia, Supplemento, 1953. Societa Italiana di Gerontologia e Geriatria Florence, Italy

Ha'agudah ha-Israelit le 'Gerontologyah Yedion, 1965 Tel Aviv, Israel (see *Israel Gerontological Society Information Bulletin*)

Indian Geriatrics Journal, 1964. Indian Geriatrics Centre, Ludhiana, India

Indian Journal of Gerontology, 1969. Indian Gerontological Association, Jaipur, India

International Association of Gerontology Bulletin, 1959. (Supplement to *Giornale di Gerontologia*)

Israel Gerontological Society Information Bulletin, 1965. Israel Gerontological Society, Tel Aviv, Israel *(Ha'agudah ha-Israelit le 'Gerontologyah Yedion)*

Japanese Journal of Geriatrics, 1964. (see *Nippon Ronen Igakkai Zasshi*) Japanese Geriatrics Society, Tokyo, Japan

Journal of the American Geriatrics Society, 1946 and 1953. (see *Geriatrics*) American Geriatrics Society, Inc., New York, New York

Journal of Geriatric Dentistry, 1966. American Society for Geriatric Dentistry, Chicago, Illinois

Journal of Geriatric Psychiatry, 1967. Boston Society for Gerontologic Psychiatry, International University Press, New York, New York

Journal of Gerontology, 1946. Gerontological Society, Inc., Washington, D.C.

Journal of Gerontology, 1956. American Osteopathic Academy of Geriatrics (Dc)

Journées Internationalles de Travail en Gérontologie Sociale, 1968. Sociadad Venezilana de Geriatrie y Gerontologie, Caracas, Venezuela

Korei Agaku, 1957–1970. (see *Geriatric Medicine*) Tokyo, Raifo Ekusutenshone Kenkyusho, Tokyo, Japan

Nippon Ronen Igakkai Zasshi, 1964. (see *Japanese Journal of Geriatrics*)

Revista Espanola de Gerontologia, 1965. Sociedad Espanola de Gerontologia, Madrid, Spain

Voprosy Gerontologii i Geriatrii, 1962. Akademiia Meditsinkikh Nauk SSSR; Institut Gerontologii 1 Eksperimental noi Patologii, Kiev, USSR

Yokufukai Geriatric Journal, 1930 (formerly, *Acta Gerontologica Japonica*), Yokufukai Geriatric Hospital, Tokyo, Japan [see text]

Yokufuen Chosa Kenkyu Kiyo, 1931, 2nd issue, (see *Acta Gerontologica Japonica*) [see text]
Zeitschrift für Gerontologie, 1968 Europaeische Zeitschrift für Altersmedizin und interdisziplinaere Alternsforschung Oesterreichische; Deutsche Gesellschaft für Gerontologie und die Oesterreichischen Gesellschaft für Geriatrie, Darmstadt, West Germany
Zikna, 1972. Israel Gerontological Society, Tel Aviv, Israel

SOCIAL AND GOVERNMENT AGENCIES

Added Years, 1959–1972. New Jersey State Office on Aging Newsletter, Trenton, New Jersey
Age in Action, 1966. West Virginia Commission on Aging, Charleston, West Virginia
Aging, 1951 (suspended 1952, resumed 1953). United States Department Health, Education, and Welfare, Administration on Aging, Washington, D.C.
Age in Connecticut, 1958–1961. Connecticut Commission on Services for Elderly Persons and the Institute of Gerontology, University of Connecticut, Storrs, Connecticut
Aging in Metropolitan St. Louis, 1959. Health and Welfare Council of Metropolitan St. Louis, Missouri
Aging in Michigan, 1961. Michigan Commission on Aging, Lansing, Michigan
Aging in the News, 1963. Wisconsin State Division on Aging, Commission on Aging, Madison, Wisconsin
Aging in Virginia, 1959. Commission on the Aging, Richmond, Virginia
Age Wise, 1959–1965. Florida Council on Aging, Tallahassee, Florida
Apex, 1974. California Office on Aging, Sacramento, California
Better Tomorrows, 1961, n.s. 1975. Utah State Division of Aging, Department of Social Security, Salt Lake City, Utah
California Senior Citizen News, 1961. Senior Citizen's Service Association, Pasadena, California
Cameo Newsletter, 1962–1970. New York State Office for the Aging, Albany, New York

Delaware Commission for the Aging, Newsletter, n.d. Smyrna, Delaware

Dialogue, 1966. State Recreation Council for the Elderly, State Education Department, Albany, New York

Elder Statesman, 1958. (formerly, *Senior Citizens News and Pensioner*) Elder Citizens in British Columbia, Vancouver, British Columbia

ERA, 1974. Department of Aging, Sacramento, California

Gericultura, 1968. Comision Puertorriquena de Gericultura, Santurce, Puerto Rico

Gerontologie 70 (annual). Diffusion Artistique et Graphique, Les Amies de la Révue de Gérontologie, Paris, France

Growing Older, 1966. Australian Council on Ageing, Melbourne, Victoria, Australia

Helsenytt, 1910 and 1963. *(Meddelelser)* Nasjonalforeningen for Folkehelsen, Oslo, Norway

Horizons, 1968. Human Resources Development Department, Alberta Council on Aging, Edmonton, Alberta, Canada

Industrial Gerontology, 1969. National Council on the Aging, Washington, D.C.

Later Years, 1958. Advisory Committee for the Care of the Aged (see under Organizations)

Lay Advocate News, 1973. New York City Office for Aging, New York, New York

Leef Tijd, 1963. (see *Op Leeftijd*)

Longevita, 1952–1961. Centro Nazionale di Gerontologia, Milan, Italy

Louisiana Senior Citizen, 1970–1973. Louisiana Commission on Aging, Baton Rouge, Louisiana

Mature Living, 1959. Indiana State Commission on the Aging and Aged, Indianapolis

Mature Living, n.d. Iowa State Commission on the Aging and the Aged, Des Moines, Iowa

Mature Years, 1954. (supersedes *Home Quarterly*) Methodist Publishing House, Nashville, Tennessee

Mature Years, New Directions, 1962. Connecticut State Commission on Services for Elderly Persons, Connecticut Department on Aging, Hartford, Connecticut

Maturity; Newsletter, 1954–1966. (superseded by *Senior Californian*) Sacramento, California

Meddelelser, 1910–1963. (see *Helsenytt* and text:)
National Council on the Aging (NCOA) Journal, 1965 (title varies). National Council on the Aging, Washington, D.C.
NCOA Journal (see above)
Nederlands tijdschrift voor Gerontologie, 1970. Deventer Nederlandse Vereniging voor Gerontologie, The Hague, Netherlands
New York City Office for the Aging Reporter, 1969. New York, New York
New York State Office for the Aging Newsletter, 1975. Albany, New York
Norske Gerontologiske Skrifter, 1955. Norsk Selskap for Altersforskning, Oslo, Norway (see *Meddelelser*)
Òp Leeftijd, 1963. Nederlandse Federatie voor Bejaardenbeleid, The Hague, Netherlands (see *Leef Tijd*)
Open Venster: Maandblad Voor Ouderen, 1957. Boekencentrum B.V., The Hague, Netherlands
Options: News for Older New Yorkers, 1974. New York City Office for the Aging, New York, New York
Pakistan Journal of Geriatrics/Pakistan Probin Hitashi, 1963. Bangladesh Association for the Aged, formerly, Pakistan Association for the Aged, Dacca, Bangladesh
Pensioners Voice, 1938. National Federation of Old Age Associations, Lancashire, England
Problemi Na Gerontologiiata I Geriatriiata, 1965. Tsentur Po Gerontologiia I Geriatriia, Sofia, Bulgaria
Pro Senectute, 1923. Schweiz Zeitschrift fuer Altersfuersorge, Alterspflege und Altersversicherung, Swiss Foundation (Pro Senectute; Schweizerische Stiftung Für das Altern; Fondation Suisse pour la Vieillesse *(Zeitlupe)*, Zurich, Switzerland
Rapport fran Institutet for Gerontologie Jönköping, 1970. (see *Skrifter Utgivna*)
Rassegna Geriatrica, 1965. Istituto Nazionale di Riposo e Cura per Anziani, Ancona, Italy
Retirement Administrators' Newsletter, 1963. Retirement Council, Stamford, Connecticut
Retirement Advisor, 1959. (title varies: *Retirement Counsellor, Retirement Advisors,* Inc.), New York, New York
Senior Californian, 1968. (superseded Commission's *Maturity; Newsletter*), California Commission on Aging, Sacramento, California

Senior Citizen, 1955. Senior Citizens of America, Washington, D.C.

Senior Citizen, 1963. Senior Citizens in Action, Inc., Los Angeles, California

Senior Citizens Activities, 1959. Bureau of Parks and Recreation, St. Paul, Minnesota

Senior Citizens Gazette, 1974. Nassau County Department of Recreation and Parks, East Meadow, New York

Senior Citizens News, 1970. Montana Commission on Aging, Social and Rehabilitation Service Department, Helena, Montana

Senior Citizens News, 1964. National Council of Senior Citizens, Inc., Washington, D.C.

Senior (Citizen) News/Senior Nuus, 1968. South African National Council for the Welfare of the Aged, Cape Town, South Africa

Senior Citizens Post, 1971. Coordinating Council of Senior Citizens, Durham, North Carolina

Senior Newsletter, 1973. Washington State Office on Aging, Olympia, Washington

Senior Sentinel, 1975. West Central Area Agency on Aging, Abilene, Texas

Seniors in Sacramento, 1972. California Rural Legal Assistance Program, Sacramento, California

Skrifter Utgivna av Institutet för Gerontologie i Jönköping, 1969. (merged *Rapport fran Institutet for Gerontologie Jönköping,* 1970) Göteborg, Sweden

United Senior Citizens of Ontario Bulletin, 1969. United Senior Citizens of Ontario, Canada (changed to *Voice of United Senior Citizens of Ontario*), Ontario, Canada

Vivre Longtemps/On Growing Old, 1957. Canadian Council on Social Development, Canadian Welfare Council, Committee on Aging, Ottawa, Canada

Voice of United Senior Citizens of Ontario, 1969. (see *United Senior Citizens of Ontario Bulletin*)

Washington State Department of Social and Health Services, 1958. Office on Aging, Senior Newsletter, Olympia, Washington

Zeitlupe; das Senioreu-Magazin, 1923. (see *Pro Senectute*)

PUBLICATIONS

Advances in Gerontological Research, 1964. Academic Press, New York, New York

Age of Achievement, 1970. Age of Achievement, Inc., Seattle, Washington

Aging, 1975. Raven Press, New York, New York

Aging and Human Development, 1970. An International Journal of Psycho-social Gerontology, (see *International Journal of Aging and Human Development*) Baywood Publishing Company (Greenwood Periodicals), Westport, Connecticut

Altenheim, 1962. (title varies: *Altersheim, Das Altenheim* 1962 q.v.) C.R.N. Vincentz, Berlin, West Germany

Altern, 1972. Springer, Berlin, West Germany

Bejaarden, 1954. (superseded by *Vakblad de Bejaarden*)

Chronic Disease Management, 1971. (formerly *Geriatric Times*) Edwill Pub, New York, New York

Excerpta Medica, Section 20, Gerontology and Geriatrics, 1958. Excerpta Medica Foundation, Amsterdam and New York

Experimental Aging Research, 1975. EAR Inc, Mt Desert, Maine

Experimental Gerontology, 1964. Pergamon Press, Inc., New York and Oxford, England

Geriatric Care, 1969. K. Eymann, Minneapolis, Minnesota

Geriatric Focus, 1962. Geriatric Focus Publications, Inc. Orange, New Jersey (Dc)

Geriatric Medicine/Ronen Igaku 1971. (see *Kindai Igakusha/Korei Igaku, Tokyo,* 1957) Yen Life Science Co, Tokyo, Japan

Geriatric Nursing, 1965–1968. Miller Publishing Company, Minneapolis, Minnesota

Geriatric Opinion, 1968. Opinion Publications, Inc., Framingham, Massachusetts

Geriatric Times, 1967–1970. (superseded by *Chronic Disease Management*) Edwill Publ., New York

Geriatrics, 1946. Lancet Publications (see *Journal of the American Geriatrics Society*), Minneapolis, Minnesota

Geriatrics, 1968. *Modern Geriatrics, Modern Medicine of Great Britain,* London, England

Geriatrics: A Medical World News Publ, 1971. New York, New York

Geriatrics, Tokyo, 1957–1964. (see *Ronenbyo*)
Geriatrics Digest, 1964. Geriatrics Digest, Inc., Northfield, Illinois
Geriatrics Marketeer, 1961. Geriatric Magazines of Minneapolis, Minneapolis, Minnesota
Gerontologia, 1957. International Society of Gerontological Research, S. Karger, Basel, Switzerland
Gerontologia Clinica, 1959. Internationale Zeitschrift fuer Geriatrie, International Journal of Gerontology, Journale Internationale de Geriatrie, S. Karger, Basel, Switzerland
Gerontological Nursing, 1975. CP Slack, Thorofare, New Jersey
Gerontology, 1970 (one issue). Iliffe Science and Technology Publications, Guildford, England
Gerontology and Geriatrics, 1958 (see *Excerpta Medica, Section 20*)
Gerontologie en Geriatrie, 1968. Bijdragen vit de praktijk, Dekker & Van de Vegt, Nijmegen, Nederlands
Harvest Years, 1960 (preview issue). Name changed to *Retirement Living,* 1972 q.v., Harvest Years Publ., New York, New York
Human and Animal Aging, 1972. Biosciences Information Service of Biological Abstracts, Philadelphia, Pennsylvania
Human Development, 1958. (formerly *Vita Humana*) Internationale Zeitschrift für Lebensaltersforschung. International Journal of Human Development. Journal Internationale de developpement humain, S. Karger, Publ., Basel, Switzerland
International Journal of Aging and Human Development, 1973. (continues as *Aging and Human Development*), Baywood Publ, Farmingdale, New York
International Journal of Experimental and Clinical Gerontology, 1976. (Merger of *Gerontologia* and *Gerontologia Clinica*) S Karger, Basel, Switzerland
International Journal of Gerontological Research, 1957. S. Karger, Publ., Basel, Switzerland
Journal of Geriatrics, 1970. Australian Geriatrics Publishing Co., Artarmon Australia
Journal of Gerontological Nursing, 1975 (see *Geriatric Nursing*)
Journal of Lifetime Living, 1955. (see *Lifetime Living, Journal of Living,* 1935–1955) absorbed, *Lifetime Living,* 1955 (see

Modern Maturity, formed by merger of *Lifetime Living and Journal of Living,* 1955) New York, New York

Journal of Living, 1955 (see *Journal of Lifetime Living*)

Kindai Igakusha Korei Igaku, Tokyo, 1957 (see *Geriatric Medicine,* Tokyo)

Lifetime Living, 1955. (see *Journal of Lifetime Living*)

Long Life, 1895. (see text)

Longevity, 1896. (see text)

Long Term Care, 1976. Washington Report, McGraw-Hill, New York, New York

Mechanisms of Ageing and Development, 1972. Association for the Advancement of Aging Research, Elsevier Sequoia, Lausanne, Switzerland

Medicina Geriatrica, 1969. Associazione Medici Geriatri Italiani, Florence, Italy

Modern Geriatrics, 1970. *Geriatrics, Modern Medicine of Great Britain,* London, England

Notre Temps, 1968. G. Lacorre, Paris, France

Referatovy Vyber z Gerontologie a Geriatrie (Abstracts of Gerontology and Geriatrics ... formerly *Referatovy Vyber z Geriatrie*) 1968. Ustav pro Zdravotnickou Dokumentacni a Knohiovnickori Sluzbu, Prague, Czechoslovakia

Retirement, "in the interest of mellow years folk, middle age and beyond," 1955. Springfield, Massachusetts

Retirement Living, 1960. (continues *Harvest Years*) *Harvest Years/Retirement Living,* 1968, Harvest Years Publ., New York, New York

Retirement Planning News, 1956–1964. (absorbed by *Retirement Living*) Retirement Council of New York, New York, New York

Revue Francaise de Gérontologie, 1954. (see *Revue de Gérontologie d'Expression Francaise*) Editions de la Vie Médicale, Paris, France

Revue de Gérontologie d'Expression Francaise: Revue Francaise de Gérontologie, 1954. v s

Ronen Igaku, 1971. (see *Geriatric Medicine*) Yen Life Science Company, Tokyo, Japan

Ronenbyo (Geriatrics), 1957–1964. *Kanehara Shuppan K.K.,* Tokyo, Japan

Senior Citizen News, 1973. John Clay Portland, Oregon

Senior Citizens Today, 1971. C.W. Skoien, Jr., Sacramento, California

Senior World, 1973. Senior World Publications, San Diego, California

Vakblad de Bejaarden, 1954. (formerly *Bejaarden*) C. de Boer, Hilversum, Netherlands

Vita Humana, 1958 (see *Human Development*)

Zeitschrift für Alternsforschung, 1938. (suspended 1944–1951) Gesellshaft fuer Gerontologie der DDR, Dresden, East Germany, (see text)

Zeitschrift für Praeklinische Geriatrie; Medizin des Alternden, 1970. Straube, Erlängen, West Germany

ORGANIZATIONS

AARP News Bulletin, 1958. American Association of Retired Persons, Washington, D.C.

Adding Life to Years, 1954–1971. (title varied: *Iowa University Institute of Gerontology Bulletin*), Iowa City, Iowa

Ageing International, 1974. International Federation on Ageing, Washington, D.C.

Aging and Development, 1971. (see *Altern und Entwicklung*)

Aging 1975. (see *Bulletin on Aging*)

Aging Highlights, 1960. (irregular) APWA Project on Aging, Chicago, Illinois

Altern und Entwicklung/Aging and Development, 1971. Kommission für Alternsforschung und Kommission für Humansforschung, Akademie der Wissenschaften und der Literatur, Mainz, Germany

Aspects of Aging, 1959. Central Bureau for Jewish Aged, New York, New York

Black Aging, 1975. National Council on Black Aging, Inc., Durham, North Carolina

Bulletin on Aging, 1975. Newsletter, Social Development Division of the United Nations Secretariat, New York, New York

Das Altenheim, 1962. (formerly *Altersheim,* title varies) Organ der Gemeinnuetziegen und Privaten Alten, Berlin, West Germany

De Aeldres Levevilkar, 1965, Kobenhavn Teknisk Forlag, Socialforskningsinstituttet, Copenhagen, Denmark

Deutsche Gesellshaft fuer Gerontologie Veroeffentlichungen, 1968–1970. Steinkopff, Darmstadt, Germany

Dynamic Maturity, 1965. American Association of Retired Persons, Long Beach, California

Ebenezer, 1934. Ebenezer Society, Minneapolis, Minnesota

L'Echo des Vieux de France, 1946. (started in 1945) Union des Vieux de France, Paris, France

Elder Care, 1968–1970. Pennsylvania Association of Nursing and Convalescent Homes, Erie, Pennsylvania.

Geriatric Institutions, 1955. National Geriatrics Society, (discontinued), Philadelphia Pennsylvania

Geriatrie, 1960. Anschrift der Schrifterlung, Erlangen, West Germany

Gerontologie en Geriatrie, 1968. Bijdragen uit de Praktijk, Nijmegen, Netherlands

Gerontology and Geriatrics, annual, (see *Gerontologiia i Geriatriia), Kiev, USSR*

Gray Panther News, 1975. Gray Panthers, Philadelphia, Pennsylvania

Growing Older, 1966. Australian Council on the Ageing, Melbourne, Australia

Human Development in Action, 1946. Human Development in Action Foundation, Flossmoore, Illinois

Industrial Gerontology, 1969. National Council on the Aging, Washington, D.C.

Later Years:Newsletter, 1957. Advisory Committee on the Care of the Aged, Wellington, New Zealand

Lifespan, 1967. Foundation for Aging Research, New York, New York

Lifetime Living, 1952–1954 (absorbed by *Journal of Lifetime Living*), New York, New York

Mature Years, 1954. Methodist Publishing House, Nashville, Tennessee (supersedes *Home Quarterly*)

Methodist Homes Quarterly, 1951. United Methodist Homes of New Jersey, Ocean Grove, New Jersey

Modern Maturity, 1958 (see *Journal of Lifetime Living*) American Association of Retired Persons, Long Beach, California

National Geriatrics Society Newsletter, 1962. National Geriatrics Society, Philadelphia, Pennsylvania

Newsletter, 1954. Retired State Government Employee Association of California, Sacramento, California

NRTA Journal, 1950. National Retired Teachers Association, Ojai, California (title varies)

NRTA News Bulletin, 1959 (v.s.)

Nursing Homes, 1952. American Nursing Home Association, Washington, D.C.

Old Age Pensioners, 1944–1950. Ohio Society of Old Age Pensioners, Mansfield, Ohio

Old Folks' Historical Record, 1874–1875. RC Hite publ, Memphis, Tennessee (see text)

Oldsters, 1954. Wisconsin State Department of Public Welfare, Madison, Wisconsin

Perspective on Aging, 1972. National Council on the Aging, Washington, D.C.

Protectio Vitae, 1971. Hannover, West Germany, G. Pinkvoss (continued from *Vitalstoffe-Zivilisationskrankheiten*)

Retirement Life, 1954. National Association of Retired Civil (Federal) Employees, Washington, D.C.

Retiro Azucarero, 1959. Caja del Seguro Social de los Trabajadores Azucareros, Havana, Cuba

Revista Brasileira de Geriatrica e Gerontologia, Rio de Janeiro, Brazil

Revista de Geriatria, 1955. Sociedad Lagunera de Geriatria of Mexico, Torreon, Mexico

Rivista de Gerontologia e Geriatria, 1951–1963. Rome, Italy Casilla Le Correo, Correo Central, Dir. J. Paccioni

Revista Para Jubilados y Pensionados, 1975. Buenos Aires, Argentina

Senior Citizens Reporter, n.d. Council of Golden Ring Clubs of New York City, New York

Seniors in Sacramento, 1972. California Rural Legal Assistance, Sacramento, California

Vejecia, 1958. Patronato Nacional de Ancianos e Invalidos, Caracas, Venezuela

Vita Humana, 1958–1966 (see *Human Development*)

Vitalstoffe-Zivilisationskrankheiten, 1956–1970 (see *Protectio Vitae*)

Voix du Rétraite, 1919. Societé de Presse, d'Édition et de Diffusion d'Information Sociales (combined in 1921 under same title), Paris, France (see text)

Sources

Armed Forces Medical Library Catalog 1950–1954. Ann Arbor, Michigan, JW Edwards, 1955

Biomedical Serials 1950–1960. Washington, DC, LM Spanier, US Department Health Education Welfare, Public Health Service, National Library Medicine, 1962

Biosis List of Serials. Philadelphia, Pennsylvania, BioSciences Information Service, 1972

Bowker Serials Bibliography Supplement. New York, New York. RR Bowker, 1971, 1972, 1973, 1974, 1975, 1976

Current Literature on Aging. Washington, DC, National Council on Aging Inc, 1957

Current Publications of Gerontology and Geriatrics (ed NW Shock). *J Geront,* 1948–

Excerpta Medica Sect XX Gerontology and Geriatrics. New York & Amsterdam, Internat Med Abst Serv, Excerpta Medica, 1958–

Index National Library of Serial Titles. Bethesda, Maryland, United States Dept Health Education Welfare, Nat Inst Health, DHEW, publ No. NIH 73-314, 1972

International Directory of Gerontology. Bethesda, Maryland, United States Dept Health Education Welfare, Publ Health Serv, Nat Inst Health, Nat Inst Child Health Human Dev, 1968

Irregular Serials and Annuals 1971–1972. New York, RR Bowker, 1972

Irregular Serials and Annuals 1977–1978. New York & London, RR Bowker, 1978

Librarians' Handbook. Birmingham, Alabama, EBSCO Subscription Services, 1973–

National Library of Medicine Catalog 1955–1959. Washington, DC, Judd and Detweiler, 1960

National Library of Medicine Catalog 1960–1961. Washington DC, Rowman and Littlefield, 1966

National Library of Medicine Catalog 1965–1970. Bethesda, Maryland, United States Dept Health Education Welfare, Publ Health Serv, Nat Inst Health, National Library of Medicine, 1970

National Library of Medicine Catalog 1971–1975 and annual accumulation

New Serial Titles vol 1-5 1950–1970. Library of Congress, New York & London, RR Bowker, 1973

New Serial Titles 1971–1975. Library of Congress, Washington DC, 1976

New Serial Titles 1976. Library of Congress, Washington DC, 1977

Serline. Dept Health Education Welfare, Publ Health Serv, Nat Lib Med, May 2, 1977

Shock NW: Classified Bibliography of Geriatrics and Gerontology 1949–1955. Stanford, California, Stanford Univ Press, 1957

Shock NW: Classified Bibliography of Geriatrics and Gerontology 1955–1961. Stanford, California, Stanford Univ Press, 1963

Ulrich's International Periodicals Directory 1971–1977. New York & London, RR Bowker, 1977

Ulrich's International Periodicals Directory 1977–1978. 17th ed (ed EB Titus) New York, Xerox Publ, 1977

Ulrich's Quarterly and Supplement to Ulrich's International Periodicals Directory and Irregular Serials and Annuals. New York & London, RR Bowker, 1977

Union List of Serials in Libraries of the United States and Canada. vol 1-5, 3rd ed, New York, HW Wilson, 1965

WIM 11 List of Biomedical Serials. John Crerar Library, Chicago, Illinois. Management Offices, 1975

World List of Scientific Periodicals 1900–1960. 4th ed (ed P Brown & GB Stratton), Washington DC, Butterworths, 1963

Appreciation is expressed to the Library of the College of Physicians of Philadelphia, Scott Library of Thomas Jefferson University School of Medicine, the New York Academy of Medicine, the National Institute on Aging's Gerontology Research Center in Baltimore, Maryland, the Bibliothéque Nationale in Paris, and to many editors, publishers, and others in the United States and in other countries for assistance freely given and responses to inquiries genuinely met.

Subject Index

human milk, 81, 107 *See also,* Cranach's
Fountain of Youth, 36
nutrition and, 107
physiologic particles in virginal breath,
81
sleeping between two maidens, 81
Renaissance, 34, 36
Res Romanae, 24
Retardation of Old Age, the, *See,* Bacon,
Friar Roger
Rome, 22, 24
family life, 24
influence, 24, 26
physicians' roles, 24
ruling body of Senate, 24
Rule of health by Plutarch, 23

Salerno, 27, 103
health center, 27
salernitan writings, 27
teaching center, 27
Scholasticism, development of, 31
Scientific Learning and Communication,
Period of, 42
Scrofula, touched for, 40
Senate, Roman, 24, 25
Senectitude, 59
Senescence, 82
Senescence, attritional aspects, 36, 45
Senility, beginning of, 45
Senility, Origin of, 137
Sexual vigor and aging, 36, 107
Shakespeare's old people, 40, 42
Smith, Captain John, 130
Soma, 19
Sources, 153–155
Sparta, 23
its gerousia, ruling body, 23
Struldbrugs, 104
Sudorifics in Egyptian medicine, 21
and longevity, 21
Surgery in the aged, 45
danger of, 45
Swiss Foundation for the Aging, 134, 135,
136 *See also* Pro Senectute

Taboos about health, 16
Tao, Taoism, 18
Yin and Yang principle, 18
Temperance, 107
Temple of Health, 126
Temple of Hymen, 126
Tobacco, use of, 40

Universities, 32
Ur, 21
Uxudo, 21

Vidary, powdered bulb, 19
Western culture, 34
White House Conference on Aging, 1961, 139
Wicket, Bostwickian, 55
Yin and Yang, 18
Yokufukai (Institution for the Elderly in
Japan), 135

NAME INDEX

Adam (Genesis 2; age 930), 21, 104
Addison, Joseph (1672–1719), 37, 38
Aesculapius, Rome's God of Medicine, 20,
103
Aivazov, Makhmud (said to be 148 years of
age), 52
Alexander the Great, or III (356–323 B.C.), 24
Amako, F. (d. 1972), 135
American Geriatrics Society 1942
Aretaeus of Cappadocia (81–?138), 24
Aristotle, the Stagirite (ca. 384–322 B.C.), 22,
24, 27, 80
Arnaldus de Villanova (?1235–1311), 27, 28,
29, 30, 80
Asklepiads, Grecian health officers, 23
Asklepieia, Gracian health centers, 23, 103
Asklepios, Greece's God of Medicine, 20, 23
Avicenna, Persian Prince of Medicine
(980–1037), 27

Bacon, Sir Francis (1561–1626), 38, 39, 40, 43,
63
Bacon, Friar Roger (?1214–1294), 32, 80
Basilevich, Ivan (1899–1965), 138
Beauvoir, Simone de (1909–   ), *Intro* 11
Bellay of Lyon, France (fl. 18th c.), 125
Besredka, Alexander C. (1870–1940), 137
Bichat, Marie-Francois Xavier (1771–1802),
43
Boerhaave, Hermann (1668–1738), 81
Bogomolets, Alexander A. (1881–1946), 59,
138
Bostwick, Homer (fl. 19th C.), 55
Brion of Lyon, France (fl. 18th c.), 125
Browning, Robert (1812–1889), 115
Buffon, Comte de, Georges Leclerc
(1707–1780), 43
Burstein, Sona Rosa (1897–1971), 58

Canstatt, Carl (1807–1850), *Intro* 10, 45
Carlisle, Sir Anthony (1768–1840), 45
Carlson, Anton Julius (1875–1956), 137–138

McCay, Clive M. (1898–1967), 58
Miles, Walter R. (1885–1978), 48
Minot, Charles Sedgwick (1852–1914), 47
Moses ben Maimon, called Maimonides
   (1135–1204), 27, 28
Moses (Exodus), 21, 30
Mueller-Deham, Albert (1881–1971), 58, 59

Napoleon I (1769–1821), 27
Nascher, Ignatius Leo (1863–1944), 16, 48, 58,
   83, 103, 130, 133
Nestor, Grecian noble warrior, 23
Nikitin, Vladimir N. (1908–   ), 58

Osler, William (1849–1919), 20, 48, 58, 59

Parr, Thomas (ca. 1483–1635), 38, 48, 53, 80,
   104
Peale, Charles Willson (1741–1827), 59
Pearl, Raymond (1879–1940), 137
Pereira, Javier (1789–1956), 52, 104
Plato (?427–347 B.C.), 23, 24, 36
Ploucquet, William Godfrey de (1744–1814),
   58
Plutarch, the biographer (?461?120 A.D.), 23
Pocahontas (?1595–1617), 130
Polonius, father of Laertes (Shakespeare's
   Hamlet), 59
Ponce de Leon (?1460–1521), 81
Pope Sixtus IV (1414–1484) papacy
   (1471–1484), 32, 33
Priam, last King of Troy, 23
Prus, Clovis René (1793–1850), 45
Pythagoras (182–?507 B.C.), 19

Quetelet, Lambert Adolphe Jacques
   (1796–1874), 49, 83

Rabson, Milton S. (1901–   ), 58
Rameses II (?1304–?1237 B.C.), 21
Ranchin, Francois (1560–1641), 40, 55, 56
Rembrandt van Rijn (1606–1669), 115
Rush, Benjamin (1745–1813), 43

Sanctorius, Sanctorius (1561–1636), 38, 49
Seidel, August (1863–?), 46
Shakespeare, William (1564–1616), 39, 40
Shaw, George Bernard (1855–1950), 115
Shock, Nathan W. (1906–   ), *Intro* 11
Sinclair, Sir John (1754–1835), *Intro* 10, 44,
   53, 54, 58, 81, 104
Smith, Charlie (said to be 132 years of age
   in 1978), 104
Smith, Captain John (1580–1631), 130
Smith, John (?1630–1670), 40, 130
Solomon (*see* Koheleth), 22
Socrates, Greek philosopher (?469–399 B.C.),
   23
Stephens, Charles Asbury (1845–1931), 46,
   103, 128, 129
Steudel, Johannes (1901–1973), 58
Stieglitz, Edward J. (1899–1956), 59
Sushruta, disciple of Dhanvantari (5th c.
   A.D.), 19, 81
Swift, Jonathan (1667–1745), 104

Taylor, Thomas (1758–1835), 80
Thévenin, health officer of Lyon, France (fl.
   18th C.), 125
Thewlis, Malford (1889–1956), 58, 83, 138
Thoms, William John (1803–1885), 48, 53
Tintoretto (1518–1594), 36
Tithonus, son of the King of Troy, mortal
   husband of Eos, 49
Titian (1477–1566), 36
Trollope, Anthony (1815–1882), 48, 59

Venner, Tobias (1577–1660), 40
Villanova, Arnaldus de (*see,* Arnaldus de
   Villanova)
Vischer, Adolph Lucas (1884–?), 58

Warthin, Alfred Scott (1866–1931), 48

Zeman, Frederic D. (1894–1970), 58, 83
Zerbi, Gabrielle (?1445–1505), 32, 33
Zeus, Grecian king of the gods, 49